How to use Roth and IRA accounts to provide a secure retirement 2018 Edition

by

Michael Gray, CPA with Thi T. Nguyen, CPA

ISBN 978-0-9967081-9-7

Copyright Notices

LEGAL NOTICES:

While all attempts have been made to provide effective, verifiable information in this book, neither the author nor publisher assumes any responsibility for errors, inaccuracies, or omissions. Any slights of people or organizations are unintentional.

If advice concerning tax, legal, compliance, or related matters is needed, the services of a qualified professional should be sought. This publication is designed to provide accurate and authoritative information in regard to the subject matter covered. It is sold with the understanding that the publisher is not engaged in rendering legal, accounting, or other professional service. If legal advice or other expert assistance is required, the services of a competent professional person should be sought.

Since federal and local laws differ widely, as do codes of conduct for members of professional organizations and agencies, the licensee must accept full responsibility for determining the legality and/or ethical character of any and all business transactions and/or practices adopted and enacted in his or her particular field and geographic location, whether or not those transactions and/or practices are suggested, either directly or indirectly, in this book.

As with any business advice, the reader is strongly encouraged to seek professional counsel before taking action. NOTE: No guarantees of savings or profits are intended by this book. Many variables affect each individual's results. Your results will vary from the examples given.

Michael Gray, CPA has no control over what you may do or not do with this book, and therefore cannot accept the responsibility for your results. You are the only one who can initiate action in order to reap your own rewards!

You are hereby advised that any written tax advice contained in this communication was not written or intended to be used (and cannot be used) by any taxpayer for the purpose of avoiding penalties that may be imposed under the U.S. Internal Revenue Code.

Published by:
Silicon Valley Publishing Co.
2482 Wooding Ct.
San Jose, CA 95128-4271
United States of America
ISBN 978-0-9967081-9-7

For more information

Please direct your questions to Thi T. Nguyen, CPA, thi@koehlercpa.com.

Are you seeking a speaker for your group about IRAs and Roth IRAs? Are you seeking a resource for a story about IRAs and Roth IRAs?

Thi T. Nguyen, CPA is available for a limited number of presentations about IRAs and Roth IRAs and for media interviews. For more information, call (408)286-7400, extension 206 or write Ms. Thi T. Nguyen, CPA, Koehler & Associates CPAs, Inc., 1541 The Alameda, San Jose, CA 95126.

Gift Certificate

Praise for
How to use Roth and IRA accounts to provide a secure retirement

"Finally, a book on IRAs anyone can understand. Michael has done a great job of explaining how we all can retire and not count on Social Security. This little book contains the relevant facts about IRAs and eliminates the bible sized manuals written for CPAs. Well done."

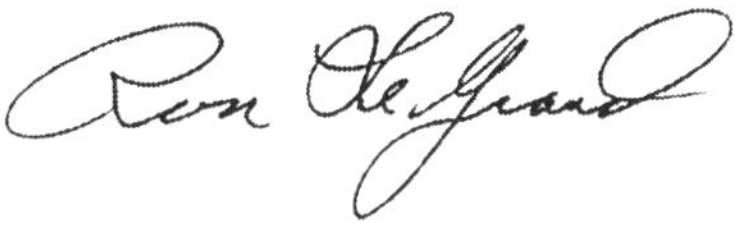

Ron LeGrand
www.ronlegrand.com

"Do these two things now to create your secure retirement nest-egg (while avoiding debilitating tax traps): buy this book and start saving regularly."

Michael J. Jones, CPA
Thompson Jones LLP
www.thompsonjones.com

"*How to use Roth and IRA Accounts to Provide a Secure Retirement* is not sales propaganda published to help the broker "make the sale." It is an investor's working manual to take charge of the conversation in order to make decisions best suited for the saver of the capital to be invested. If you are an investor, you can use this book to know what is possible, why it is possible, and how to use an IRA and/or a Roth as a building block in your financial planning.

"I also recommend this book to anyone who is interviewing for a new financial advisor and would like to ask fact based questions and not be blinded with charts and graphs giving the company line. Use the information in the book to ask the potential advisor questions they should know before you give your money over for new management. Ask yourself, can a new advisor truly help me with what is possible when the advisor has not taken the time to learn about IRAs and Roths?"

Dick Blakeley
The Blakeley Group, Inc.
www.theblakeleygroup.com

"Many individuals have recently begun to discover the 'secret' of taking advantage of certain tax benefits to maximize the return on their retirement accounts. These plans, known as Individual Retirement Arrangements (IRAs), were initially authorized pursuant to the Employee Retirement Income Security Act (ERISA) when it was signed into law on Labor Day, 1974, so IRAs have been around for a while. However, relatively few individuals – accountants, lawyers, and financial planners among them – really understand how IRAs work and how they can be used to maximum advantage in retirement planning. After all, the regulations were created by both the Department of Labor and the Department of the Treasury, so some degree of complexity would be expected. Michael Gray, a Certified Public Accountant, has successfully compiled a practical overview of the key points of these regulations into a concise summary that anyone can use to learn the basics about this otherwise obscure retirement planning tool. Of course, you should consult with a knowledgeable financial planning, tax, and legal advisor before making any investment choices. But reading Michael Gray's book will put you well ahead of the curve in your ability to ask the right questions and make intelligent financial decisions for your retirement."

Jeffrey B. Hare, Attorney at Law
jeff@jeffreyhare.com

"Michael Gray is a highly-respected tax professional who brings decades of practical experience to his writings. His latest publication, *How to use Roth and IRA Accounts to provide a secure retirement, 2012 Edition*, is a comprehensive consumer guide to maximizing the tax benefits available to all of us through proper handling of retirement accounts. As the author demonstrates, there is much more to managing a retirement account than simply selecting investments. Planning regarding rollovers, distributions and beneficiary designations significantly impacts the tax burdens borne by these assets. Mr. Gray's book is a fabulous resource."

Naomi S. Comfort, Esq., JD, LLM Tax
Silicon Valley Elder Law, PC
naomi@svelaw.com

"The world of retirement accounts can be complex and mysterious to the average investor or retirement saver. This work by Michael Gray simplifies much of the jargon and complex rules. As such, the typical consumer can learn and take advantage of the positive aspects of savings vehicles, in particular, the Roth IRA that is probably the best U.S. savings vehicle ever created. Thirty per cent of the graying U.S. population has no retirement savings, and most others are insufficiently prepared. It is critical to the development of a sound private retirement system, that comprehensive and understandable educational information like Michael Gray's reach the public so that a renewed interest in saving is stimulated!"

Tom W. Anderson
President, Retirement Industry Trust Association (RITA) and
Founder and Vice Chairman
PENSCO Trust Company
www.PENSCO.com

"The book is great. It is an excellent summary of some very complex law. I love the section on Roth vs Traditional IRAs. It is the best summary explanation I have seen on the subject."

Raymond Sheffield, Esq.
Sheffield Law Office
www.sheffieldestateplanning.com

“I have known Michael Gray, CPA for most of the 35 years I have been in the financial planning and asset management business. Some of our clients are also served by Michael Gray for tax consulting and tax return preparation services. In my opinion, Mike’s clients are getting a bargain in having his professional expertise available! This new book represents a practical guide to IRA and Roth IRA decision making for the average investor. As a professional in the financial industry, I consider this book to be an invaluable resource for my desk.”

Craig Martin, MSFS, CFP, CLU, ChFC
Fee-only financial planner
The Family Wealth Consulting Group
www.fwcg.net

Contents

1
Introduction

The most significant assets of most individuals in the United States are their home and their retirement account. (High tech executives also have employee stock options, real estate investors have their real estate and other investors have their securities accounts.)

Financing a retirement can be challenging. Life expectancy keeps getting longer. According to the Society of Actuaries, there is a 45% chance that one of a married couple age 65 will live to age 90 and an 18% chance that one of them will live to age 95. That's a long time!

Baby boomers are in or approaching their retirement years. They face difficult choices about what to do with their 401(k) accounts. Should they leave them with the plan or roll them over to an IRA?

(In this book, a "Roth" account is a Roth IRA account and an "IRA" account is a regular IRA or individual retirement account. An "employer plan" is a qualified retirement plan relating to your employment, including 401(k), profit sharing, 403(b) for nonprofit, 457 for government, and other less common plans.)

During a participant's lifetime, he or she can now convert a "regular" IRA to a Roth account. In addition, some "regular" 401(k) accounts can be converted to Roth 401(k) accounts.

In this book, I intend to provide a framework for further discussion with your tax and investment advisors. I have written the book for the layperson. This is not an exhaustive, technical explanation.

I intentionally haven't extensively documented the text. The footnote references are for convenience when questions come up.

The detailed rules and choices have grown to be staggering, so I am intentionally focusing on the highlights to provide an overview. If you believe I have missed a significant area that should be included, please write to me at mgray@taxtrimmers.com and I'll consider including it in later editions of this book.

Remember to check for the state tax consequences of your transaction. Many states have tax rules that don't conform to the Internal Revenue Code. For example, California taxes long-term capital gains at the same tax rates as ordinary income.

Whenever we write about tax laws, we have a moving target. Tax laws change regularly, including new rulings by the courts and the IRS, new Treasury Regulations, and new tax laws passed by Congress. (The changes in the Tax Cuts and Jobs Act of 2017 are staggering!) Investors should consult with tax advisors about these matters. Tax advisors must be alert for developments and perform research to support their advice. One way to keep up to date is to subscribe to *Michael Gray, CPA's Tax and Business Insight* at www.taxtrimmers.com. Until further notice, there is no charge or obligation to subscribe to this email newsletter.

A big "Thank you!" to the folks who read preliminary versions of this book and gave me suggestions to improve it. Thi Nguyen, CPA, who is the successor for my former tax consulting and tax return preparation practice, is a contributor. Michael Jones, CPA has awesome technical expertise in the tax laws relating to IRAs, Roths and estate planning, so I was especially delighted that he agreed to read the text and give suggestions. Dick Blakeley volunteered to contribute a case study and Lori Greymont volunteered to contribute material about due diligence for the book. Tom Anderson, founder of PENSCO Trust Company and President of the Retirement Industry Trust Association (RITA), has a wealth of hands-on experience from which he made many valuable suggestions. Other friends who generously read the book with feedback included Ron LeGrand, Craig Martin, Naomi Comfort, Lamaar Baxter, Jeffrey Hare and Raymond Sheffield. You have a much more valuable resource in your hands thanks to their contributions.

Enjoy!

Michael Gray, CPA
February 22, 2018

2
Why a Roth or IRA is a key element in a retirement plan

Since they were introduced back in 1974, individual retirement accounts have become very significant in retirement planning. The addition of the Roth individual retirement account in 1998 has provided another important item to the retirement planning menu.

Social Security is under growing pressure because we have an aging population, including an enormous "bubble" of retirements to be funded for the "baby boom" generation. (I'm a member!) I think the likely resolution of the Social Security dilemma will be to raise the retirement age when we are eligible for full benefits. Time will tell. Social Security is a cornerstone of the U.S. retirement system and I don't see our government allowing it to become bankrupt or severely curtailing it. (The AARP won't let them!)

The U.S. government knows it can't provide a comfortable retirement for all of us, so it must encourage and subsidize private solutions. That's why we have tax incentives for employer-provided and personal (Roth and IRA) retirement plans.

Principally resulting from a huge military budget to fund overseas military operations, funding health care reform, and the tax cuts in the Tax Cuts and Jobs Act of 2017, the U.S. government is incurring record deficits, which it seems must eventually lead to higher taxes to repay.

Effective for tax years after 2017, the maximum federal income tax rate is 37%. An additional 3.8% tax on net investment income has been added to the mix as part of health care reform. (Mercifully, the net investment income tax doesn't apply to taxable income from a qualified retirement plan or an IRA.)

The reduction of federal income tax rates under the Tax Cuts and Jobs Act of 2017 means that income taxes are currently "on sale." Although this seems to reduce the incentives for sheltering income in retirement accounts, the tax cuts may not be sustainable and it makes sense to take advantage of tax-favored retirement vehicles.

The premise of an IRA and most tax-deferred retirement accounts is to postpone subjecting income to tax until retirement, when you will probably be in a lower tax bracket. Many high-income taxpayers have found that they continue to be in high tax brackets after retirement, so the premise doesn't work for them unless they can shift the funds to low-bracket family members after death or to a charity. By converting to a Roth account now, they can pay tax at lower tax rates and escape tax on future earnings and growth in the account.

By the way, the Roth account is no accident. It was a way for the U.S. government to accelerate tax revenues.

In summary, U.S. tax rates will probably increase and the federal and state governments continue to look for additional revenue sources. When providing for a long-term obligation, like funding your retirement, using a tax-free Roth account can be a great advantage.

Depending on your tax picture, regular IRA accounts also have tax advantages because of the up-front tax deduction and the ability to grow your investments, usually without paying a current tax. Having a bigger fund to work with gives you more choices of investments to make.

For taxpayers in lower tax brackets, the "saver's credit" is an additional incentive for saving using a Roth or IRA. The credit is up to 50% of a contribution of up to $2,000 (for a maximum $1,000 credit) to certain retirement accounts, including regular IRAs, Roth IRAs, 401(k)s, 403(b) annuities, a governmental 457 plan, a SIMPLE IRA, a salary reduction SEP or an ABLE account. The percentage of the retirement plan contribution for which a credit is allowed is reduced until the credit is eliminated for married taxpayers filing joint returns for 2017 with adjusted gross income (AGI) exceeding $63,000, heads of household with AGI exceeding $47,250, and all others with AGI exceeding $31,500. In order to claim the credit, you must be at least 18 years old, you may not be a full-time student and no one else may claim your personal exemption. See Publication 4703 and Form 8880 at the IRS web site, www.irs.gov.

These benefits make Roths and IRAs key elements of your retirement planning toolkit.

3
Roth or IRA?

The title of this chapter is a trick question.

Probably over a lifetime you will need to use both a Roth and an IRA.

Rules of thumb

Instead of keeping you in suspense, I'll give you some rules of thumb up front. The right decisions for you will very much depend on your individual circumstances, so I recommend that you seek help from a financial planner and/or tax consultant when making decisions relating to retirement accounts.

1. The younger you are, the more a Roth is favored. You will have more time to accumulate a bigger retirement fund through untaxed compound earnings. (But remember, your beneficiaries will also be able to spread the distribution of an inherited Roth account income tax free over their life expectancies.)

2. If you expect your marginal tax bracket to go up, a Roth is favored. It's generally better to pay taxes at lower tax brackets. (This is a big wild card. Nobody really knows what our tax system will look like in the distant future when many people will retire.)

3. If the beneficiary for the account is a charity, an IRA is favored. Charities don't pay income taxes on retirement account proceeds. You might as well get a tax deduction for the money going into a retirement account if it's ultimately going to a charity. (Choosing which assets to give to a charity is an important part of estate planning. Assets that carry ordinary income, like retirement accounts and stock options, are good choices for charitable bequests.)

4. The more other assets that you have, the more a Roth is favored. Minimum distributions aren't required for a Roth

during the lifetime of the account owner and his or her spouse. If you don't need the money, you can continue to accumulate earnings tax-free for a longer time than for a regular IRA. Minimum distributions are required starting at age 70 ½ for the account owner of a regular IRA.

5 Losing the tax deduction for a contribution to a Roth or paying a tax for a conversion to a Roth can result in a financial hardship if you don't have the cash to pay the income taxes.

6 If you have beneficiaries you care about providing for, a Roth is favored. If you don't have beneficiaries that you care about providing for, who cares about leaving a tax-free account?

7 If your beneficiaries are in higher tax brackets than you are, a Roth is favored. If you left them a taxable IRA account, they would have to pay more income taxes for distributions than you would.

Features, advantages and disadvantages of "regular" IRAs

Regular individual retirement accounts or IRAs have been with us since the 1970s.

For 2017 and 2018, a taxpayer may contribute the lesser of $5,500 or his or her earned income each year to the IRA. In addition, taxpayers who are age 50 or older may contribute an additional $1,000 "catch up" contribution each year. The contribution may be made up to the original due date for the tax year, usually April 15 of the year following the tax year. (These amounts are adjusted for inflation from time to time. Check for updates.)

A non-working spouse may also contribute to an IRA based on the earnings of his or her working spouse. Separate IRAs must be set up for each spouse.

The maximum contribution is adjusted each year for inflation. Inflation has been so low that the maximum contribution has been unchanged since 2013.

The contribution may be deductible or non-deductible. The taxpayer may simply designate that he or she is making a non-deductible contribution.

The deduction is phased out for active participants in qualified retirement accounts and for their nonworking spouses. Despite the elimination of the deduction, nondeductible contributions can still be made up to the limitation listed above less any deductible contribution that is made and allowed.

An individual is an active participant who is covered by:

1 A qualified pension, profit sharing or stock bonus plan, including 401(k)s and ESOPs;

2 A qualified (employer provided) annuity plan;

3 A tax-sheltered annuity plan (for public employees);

4 A simplified employee pension (SEP);

5 A SIMPLE plan (small business 401(k) equivalent);

6 A plan established by the United States, a state or political subdivision of a state, or by a federal or state instrumentality; or

7 An employee-only contributory plan that is exempt from tax under Internal Revenue Code Section 501(c)(18).

For 2018, the deduction is phased out for active participant taxpayers who have adjusted gross income (before the IRA deduction) of $63,000 to 73,000 for single persons and heads of household and $101,000 to $121,000 for married persons filing a joint return. (For 2017, the thresholds are $62,000 to $72,000 for singles and $99,000 to $119,000 for married, filing joint returns.) No tax deduction for a contribution to an IRA is allowed for an active participant who is a married person filing a separate income tax return.

For 2018, the deduction is phased out for nonworking spouses who are married to active participants with adjusted gross income (before the IRA deduction) from $189,000 to $199,000 on a married, filing a joint return. (For 2017, the threshold are $186,000 to $196,000.

Non-deductible contributions are reported using Form 8606. The form is cumulative, tracking non-deductible contributions for the current and previous years.

A contribution to an IRA that exceeds the contribution limit is called an excess contribution. An excess contribution is subject to a cumulative, nondeductible 6% excess contribution tax. The tax can be avoided by withdrawing the excess contribution plus any earnings on the contribution on or before the due date (including extensions) of the individual income tax return. (This is generally October 15 of the year following the year that the contribution relates to.)

The main advantage of a "regular" IRA is the tax benefit of the tax deduction for contributions helps to fund the account. For example, if you are in the 40% marginal tax bracket (you would pay 40% federal and state taxes combined on the next dollar earned), you would receive a tax benefit from a $5,000 deductible IRA contribution of $2,000. So your tax savings are providing $2,000 of the amount contributed and you are providing the other $3,000.

A second advantage of a "regular" IRA is the tax deferral (in general) for earnings and any amounts rolled over from a taxable retirement account. The account can be a "parking" place for amounts received from an employer retirement account (usually a 401(k) account) when you terminate employment. This feature lets you accumulate additional capital and gives you more alternatives for investments to make with the account.

A third advantage of "regular" IRAs is you have control of the investments that you make, and may have more and better choices than are available in an employer plan. In many cases, an employer plan will simply offer a family of funds from a mutual fund company. They might not be the funds that you would choose. With the exception of a few prohibited investments, your choices with IRAs are virtually unlimited.

Some companies offer self-directed accounts (for higher fees) that can give you this flexibility.

A nondeductible contribution to a regular IRA might provide a way to bypass the Roth contribution limit.

The nondeductible contribution also provides the tax deferral feature like a regular IRA, but only on investment returns.

For those who are charitably inclined, a taxable IRA is an excellent choice of asset for a contribution. Normally, the only way to avoid a tax effect from making a donation from the account is to make the charity a beneficiary of the account. During your lifetime, you can have the funds as a contingency account to provide for your retirement or other needs, like long-term care.

A taxpayer age 70 ½ or older may make a qualified charitable distribution from a traditional IRA or Roth IRA. The distribution is not includable in taxable gross income of the taxpayer. No tax deduction is allowed for the charitable contribution. The maximum distribution amount is $100,000 for a taxable year. (SEP IRAs and SIMPLE IRAs don't qualify for these distributions. These accounts can be rolled over to a regular IRA to avoid the exception.) The charitable distribution "counts" for meeting the required minimum distribution requirement

Some states don't recognize this exclusion. Check your local rules.

Why is the lifetime gift to charity an advantage? You bypass the 50% of adjusted gross income limit for charitable contributions (60% for tax years beginning after December 31, 2017 and before January 1, 2016.) You reduce your taxable estate. You avoid a phaseout of itemized deductions that apply to taxpayers with high adjusted gross income. (The phaseout is repealed for tax years beginning after December 31, 2017 and before January 1, 2026.) The charity gets the cash sooner.

A disadvantage of an IRA is a distribution (other than to a charity) carries taxable income.

Another disadvantage is IRAs must make required minimum distributions starting for the year the participant reaches age 70 ½. Some people don't need this taxable income.

Features, advantages and disadvantages of Roth IRA accounts.

Roth accounts were adopted in 1998. They were developed to provide another retirement planning alternative in light of the challenges for Social Security. Since there is no deduction for contributions to a Roth account, there isn't an up-front tax receipts reduction to the U.S. Treasury. Tax revenue can also be generated by conversions of regular IRA and 401(k) accounts to Roth accounts. However, the long-term benefits can be significant.

For 2017 and 2018, a taxpayer may contribute the greater of $5,500 or his or her earned income to a Roth IRA. In addition, taxpayers who are age 50 or older may contribute an additional $1,000 "catch up" contribution each year. The contribution may be made up to the original due date for the tax year, usually April 15 of the year following the tax year.

A non-working spouse may also contribute to a Roth IRA based on the earnings of his or her working spouse. Separate Roth IRAs must be set up for each spouse.

The maximum contribution is adjusted each year for inflation. Inflation has been so low that the maximum contribution has been unchanged since 2013.

Unlike regular IRA contributions, Roth contributions are allowed even when you are covered by a qualified plan at work. The contribution limit is phased out based on adjusted gross income. For 2018, the maximum contribution is phased out for single persons for modified adjusted gross income between $120,000 and $135,000, and for married persons filing joint returns, the maximum contribution is phased out for modified adjusted gross income between $189,000 and $199,000. (For 2017, the thresholds are $118,000 and $133,000 for single persons and $186,000 and $196,000 for married persons filing joint returns.)

After meeting a five-year holding period requirement, distributions from Roth IRAs are tax-free, provided they also meet one of the following requirements:

1. Made on or after the date on which the participant reaches age 59 ½;
2. Made to a beneficiary (or the participant's spouse) after the participant's death;
3. Made to a disabled participant; or
4. Used to pay up to $10,000 (lifetime limit) of "qualified first-time homebuyer expenses."

A big advantage of Roth IRAs is distributions aren't required to be made during the lifetime of the participant. (Distributions are required after the death of the participant.) That means income can be accumulated in the accounts throughout the life of the participant for tax-free distribution to beneficiaries after the death of the participant.

Another advantage is taxpayers who are over age 70 ½ who have earned income can continue contributing to a Roth IRA, but can't contribute to a regular IRA.

Inherited Roth accounts must be distributed over the life expectancy of named beneficiaries.

The myRA – a discontinued Roth choice

President Obama initiated the myRA by executive order on January 29, 2014. On July 28, 2017, the IRS announced the myRA program is being discontinued. MyRA owners are encouraged to roll their myRA accounts to regular Roth IRA accounts.

The purpose of the myRA was to enable small-dollar savers to establish a Roth IRA with a Treasury-designated custodian without paying fees or start-up costs. Participants could keep their myRA account and continue to make contributions when they changed jobs. The contribution limit is the same as for a regular Roth IRA account, generally $5,500 for 2017. Contributions to a myRA are invested in the Government Securities Investment Fund ("G Fund") previously available only to federal employees participating in a Thrift Savings Plan. Only individuals who are otherwise eligible to contribute to a Roth IRA may participate.

Individuals could participate in a myRA until the sooner of when the total value of the myRA savings bond reached $15,000 or 30 years of participation. The account can be rolled over at any time to a regular Roth IRA account with a commercial financial services provider.[1]

The myRA was an attractive way to get started in accumulating a Roth account with a better interest rate than a conventional bank savings account.

[1] RIN 1530-AA08, December 19, 2014

4
Single-person 401(k) and SEP alternatives for the Self-Employed

You will have the most investment choices if you have a large balance in your retirement account. For self-employed persons, single-person 401(k)s and Simplified Employee Pensions (SEPs) are retirement plan alternatives with the fewest compliance requirements. With these plans, self-employed persons (and their employees) can have self-directed accounts with minimal fiduciary duties.

Single-person 401(k)s

Single-person 401(k)s can be contributed to like any other 401(k) plan, but have fewer compliance requirements. Since the compliance requirements are simpler, more custodians are willing to accept these plans compared to other qualified retirement plans, including families of mutual funds and self-directed plan custodians.

The only participants of a single-person 401(k) can be the business owner and the business owner's spouse, and a partner and the partner's spouse.[2] If other employees are hired that are required to be covered by the plan, a single-person 401(k) plan will convert to a regular 401(k) plan. Employees are generally "counted" when the employee is at least age 21 and has completed one year of service (works more than 1,000 hours in a plan year). Employees covered by a collective bargaining agreement can be excluded from a 401(k) plan covering other employees.

401(k) plans that aren't single person plans can be subject to testing for non-discrimination or being "top-heavy." Alternatively, the plan can require a 3% of compensation minimum employer contribution each year to eliminate the testing requirements. These requirements raise the cost of maintaining the plan.

Single-person plans with balances of less than $250,000 also aren't required to file the annual report, Form 5500, easing the compliance burden.

---

[2] Internal Revenue Code § 401(a)(35)(E)(iv)

The maximum "employee" contribution for a 401(k) plan for 2018 is $18,500 ($18,000 for 2017), limited to 100% of compensation. An annual "catch up" contribution of up to $6,000 can also be made for 2018 and 2017 for participants who are age 50 or older.

401(k)s can also have a "profit sharing" feature, permitting larger contributions than the amounts employees can usually elect to make. The maximum contribution (including both the "employer" and "employee" contributions) for 2018 is $55,000 ($54,000 for 2017), limited to 100% of compensation, net of retirement plan deferrals.

The "employee" contribution can be designated as a non-deductible Roth contribution. The Roth portion of the account needs to be accounted for separately in order to determine how much is eventually eligible for a tax-free distribution. See the chapter on Roth conversions relating to "in plan" Roth conversions in 401(k) plans after September 25, 2010.

The "employer" contribution isn't eligible for Roth treatment.

Participant loans can be permitted from self-employed 401(k) plans, but I recommend that you avoid them. It's too easy to miss a compliance requirement, resulting in an unintentional distribution.

Also see Chapter 7 on prohibited transactions for another advantage of single-person 401(k)s.

Unlike Roth IRA accounts, Roth 401(k) accounts must begin life expectancy distributions when a participant reaches age 70 ½. The employee could and probably should elect to roll the Roth 401(k) account balance to a Roth IRA account to avoid having to make required minimum distributions.

The accounting for single 401(k) plans is more complicated than for IRAs, because the amounts must be tracked attributable to employer contributions, employee contributions, and taxable vs. Roth shares. Individuals with such plans are advised to get a third party administrator to handle the accounting.

Simplified Employee Pensions (SEPs)

A Simplified Employee Pension, or SEP, is a plan alternative for self-employed persons with very low administration costs. The trade-offs are the plans are very inflexible and contributions to employee accounts are fully vested.

The employer just adopts a model plan agreement (such as Form 5305-SEP), sets up separate IRA accounts for the employees and makes contributions to the accounts by the extended due date of his or her income tax return. For most individuals, that is up to October 15 of the year following the end of the plan year. For example, if an individual return extension is filed for 2017, the contribution must be deposited by October 15, 2018.

SEPs can also be set up for small businesses other than sole proprietorships, such as corporations, S corporations, partnerships, LLCs and LLPs. These entities can have fiscal years for which the due dates of retirement plan contributions can be different from individuals.

Unlike almost any other retirement account, a SEP can actually be adopted and funded after the year end.

An employer can't have a SEP if it has or had any other kind of qualified retirement plan.

All eligible employees must be covered by a SEP. An eligible employee (1) has reached age 21; (2) has worked for the employer three of the last five years; and (3) has received at least $600 in compensation for 2018 or 2017.

Employers can't make a SEP contribution if they have leased employees.

Employers can't discriminate in favor of highly-compensated employees, but employees covered by a collective bargaining agreement and non-resident aliens who don't have U.S. source compensation can be excluded from participating in the plan.

The maximum contribution to a SEP for 2018 is 25% of compensation for up to $275,000 of compensation, to a maximum of

$55,000 (for 2017, the thresholds are 25% for up to $270,000 of compensation to a maximum of $54,000.) Since the compensation on which the contribution is made is net of the contribution, it's effectively 20% for a self-employed person. For example, the contribution for $250,000 of compensation is $250,000 - $50,000 contribution = $200,000 net compensation X 25% = $50,000. $50,000 / $250,000 = 20%. Any limit that isn't used can be carried over to succeeding years (but the contribution for 2018 still can't exceed the $55,000 limit.)

Social Security can be taken into account (Social Security integration) when computing the SEP contribution.

Summary comparison 401(k) v. SEP

Favoring the single-person 401(k):

- Roth option for "employee" contribution.
- 100% of compensation contribution limit means a bigger contribution can be made based on less income.
- Positioning for regular 401(k) when other employees are hired.
- With a 401(k), employees can fund part of their own retirement, reducing the cost for the employer.
- 401(k) isn't subject to the tax on unrelated business taxable income for leveraged real estate.
- Employees can borrow from their 401(k) accounts. The loans are limited to the lesser of $50,000 or 50% of the present value of the participant's nonforfeitable accrued benefit. The loans must be repaid within 5 years, and the loan must be amortized on a level basis, with payments at least quarterly. (Personally, I don't recommend these loans. They have a way of blowing up on you. Unpaid loans result in taxable income and penalties.)
- 401(k) plans can hold life insurance on the employee's life. If the life insurance proceeds are payable to the employee's estate or beneficiary or the plan trustee is required to pay the proceeds to the employee's estate or beneficiary, the employee must report taxable income for each year of coverage.

Favoring the SEP:

- No requirement to file a Form 5500 until $250,000 is accumulated.
- Can have some employees without adding expensive testing and compliance requirements at the possible cost of paying more to provide benefits for employees.
- Generally, the compliance, fees and expenses are lower for SEPs than for single-person 401(k)s.

Other retirement plan alternatives

When a business has several employees, the owner should consider other retirement plan alternatives. Some alternatives include defined benefit pension plans (payout defined based on compensation history), 401(k) plans, profit sharing plans, ESOPs, and more. A customized plan using these alternatives can help control costs of the plan and maximize the benefits to the business owner. The details are beyond the scope of this book. Consult with a retirement plan specialist to customize the optimum plan for your company.

There are many more compliance requirements for these plans, so they are much more expensive to administer and have more fiduciary duties attached to them. Annual financial audits might even be required. You should definitely get help from pension specialists to design, establish and administer such a plan.

5
What kinds of investments can you make with a Roth or IRA?

There is a broad assortment of investments that can be held in a Roth or regular IRA account.

It's easier to say what can't be held than what can be held. You can't hold collectibles or life insurance contracts in a Roth or IRA.

Collectibles include works of art, rugs, antiques, metal, gems, stamps, coins, alcoholic beverages and other items specified by the IRS. Roths and IRAs may invest in US-minted gold and silver coins and coins issued under the laws of any state. IRAs may also invest in certain platinum coins and any gold, silver, platinum, or palladium bullion of a specified fineness.

Roths and IRAs aren't permitted to be shareholders of S corporations, except for bank stock held on October 22, 2004, so S corporation stock generally is not a permitted investment for a Roth or IRA. (Roths and IRAs can invest in limited liability companies (LLCs), which are generally taxed as passthrough entities like S corporations.)

Although banks and brokerage companies may offer what they call "self directed" accounts, the choices might actually be limited. There are specialized companies that permit the owner of the Roth or IRA to make a broader assortment of investments. Those companies generally charge higher fees for the service, but they do not charge commissions nor are they paid by the asset sponsors. The commissions and "load" amounts paid to brokerage companies reduces the investment yield for investments held by those companies.

In addition to the prohibited investment rules, certain transactions, such as buying and selling with related parties, are also prohibited. See Chapter 7.

Note the IRS has applied a "look through" principle to Roths and IRAs to disallow personal losses on sales of securities under the "wash sale" rules when substantially identical stock and securities are purchased in a Roth or IRA account owned by the taxpayer during the period from thirty days before to thirty days after the loss sale that would otherwise be deductible on an individual income tax return. The taxpayer's basis in the Roth or IRA account isn't adjusted for the disallowed loss. A similar theory could be applied to other transactions that haven't been specified yet.

The Roth or IRA could be required to pay income taxes on income deemed "unrelated business income," including rental income from debt-financed real estate. See Chapter 10.

Since many individuals have most of their investable assets in their retirement accounts, they should consider whether to make alternative investments with those funds. The key issues are 1) Will you have a higher return on investment on an after-tax basis compared to other alternatives?; and 2) Is the risk for this investment worth taking for the potential return? Also, be careful of asset concentration. Any investment should be part of a diversified portfolio. (Again, "unrelated business income" generated by an alternative investment may subject to a Roth or IRA income tax. See Chapter 10.)

Growing a Roth or IRA account with an interest-charge DISC

The Sixth Circuit Court of Appeals reversed the Tax Court and allowed taxpayers to use an interest-charge domestic international sales corporation (IC-DISC) to grow Roth IRA accounts. An IC-DISC is a tax benefit allowed under the Internal Revenue Code. A U.S. export company pays a statutorily-defined "commission" to the IC-DISC. The IC-DISC can accumulate up to $10 million of untaxed income. The shareholders of the IC-DISC pay an interest charge for deferred income taxes. When the IC-DISC pays accumulated earnings out to the shareholders, they are taxable as dividends. For tax-exempt entities, including IRAs and Roth IRAs, the dividends are taxed as unrelated business taxable income. (See Chapter 10.)

Summa Holdings, Inc. paid commission to JC Export, an IC-DISC. JC Export distributed the money as a dividend to JC Holding, Inc., its sole shareholder. JC Holding, Inc. paid a 33% corporate income tax on the distribution, and then distributed the balance to its two shareholders, which were Roth IRA accounts.

The Tax Court initially upheld the IRS in disallowing the arrangement, and taxing the commissions to the owners of the Roth IRA accounts. This also resulted in disallowing the deduction for the commissions for Summa Holdings, Inc. The IRS claimed in a "substance over form" argument that the arrangement allowed the Roth IRA owners to bypass the limitations on annual contributions to Roth accounts. The eventual distributions from the Roth accounts would be tax-free.

The Sixth Circuit Court of Appeals said the arrangement met the requirements under the Internal Revenue Code, and should be allowed. IC-DISCs are a creation of Congress. The Internal Revenue Code provides substance to the form of this arrangement.[3]

The Tax Court later demonstrated that it doesn't agree with the Sixth Circuit Court of Appeals. It disallowed a similar arrangement using a Foreign Sales Corporation, another tax incentive arrangement of Congress that has been discontinued. In that case, the Tax Court noted that the taxpayer didn't reside in the Sixth Circuit.[4]

The IC-DISC strategy might work, but be prepared for a legal fight with IRS if you don't reside in the Sixth Circuit. The strategy is appropriate with taxpayers involved in export sales.

Note the IRS required special disclosure for arrangements they deem to bypass the annual Roth IRA contributions limits as "listed transactions."[5] Transactions between entities owned by the Roth IRA and the owner are included in this disclosure requirement.

See Chapter 16 about Qualified Annuity Contracts, an investment alternative designed to help retirees further postpone their retirement payments from IRAs and Roths.

---

[3] *Summa Holdings, Inc. v. Commissioner*, 119 AFTR 2d 2017-787, February 16, 2017

[4] Mazzei v. Commissioner, 150 TC No. 7, March 5, 2018

[5] Revenue Procedure 2004-8

See Chapter 17 about valuation and retirement accounts. The IRS is paying more attention to this issue, which will increase the costs relating to having alternative investments in Roth and IRA accounts.

6
Look before you leap! Due diligence

Since you are dealing with your retirement nest egg and accounts that represent one of the largest shares of your net worth, realize that retirement account funds should be handled with special care.

Individuals with large retirement accounts are naturally targeted by investment advisors as prospective clients. Some of them have your best interests in mind; some do not. This has more to do with character than with licensing.

Con men and women see seniors with large retirement accounts as easy prey – sheep to be shorn! You don't want to become a statistic.

The high volatility of the stock market has driven away many investors. They are seeking alternative investments. The self-directed IRA and Roth have provided flexibility to make alternative investments. They can provide a ready source of cash for alternative investments marketed by investment brokers and advisors. Since many of these alternative investments are subject to reduced SEC disclosure and reporting regulations, it just makes it easier for the public to be more vulnerable to making investments that may not be any better than the stock market. Self-directed retirement accounts can provide the mechanism to commit financial suicide.

What can you do to protect yourself? Either you or someone you hire should investigate the legitimacy of the investments that you are making and the individuals who are operating them. This investigation is called "due diligence."

Here are some suggested due diligence steps:

If you are investing in a business that isn't publicly traded there is significant risk of business failure. The only way to reduce this risk is to own hundreds of them, as in a publicly-traded mutual fund that invests in these companies. A simple and prudent due diligence step when you are buying a piece of property is to visit it. In all cases, ask a lot of questions.

Put yourself in the role of actually running the business you are considering investing in, whether it is real estate management or executing a business plan. Then ask the obvious, which are usually the scariest questions. "Does this opportunity pass the 'smell test'?" Are you being sold the equivalent of the Brooklyn Bridge or a company where you will make a fortune selling ice boxes to Eskimos? If your intuition tells you this "opportunity" is "too good to be true," pay attention!

Study any prospectus or financial statements that are available. If you don't understand them, bring them to a CPA or financial analyst and ask for them to explain them. If the financial statements aren't audited, understand they haven't been independently verified.

Consider hiring a CPA firm to perform a pre-acquisition study to determine if the company appears to be legitimate and look for any "skeletons in the closet." Are there any unrecorded liabilities, including lease obligations, lawsuits, or warranty claims?

There are services that do background checks of people and companies. The fees are modest for online research. Also consider hiring a private investigator for a background check, including interviewing neighbors and business associates and getting credit history. If the person offering the opportunity is legitimate, he or she should readily consent to such a check and provide information to do so.

Check for current business registration with the Secretary of State. Have a title search done for real estate. Check the county recorder's office for recorded liens secured by real estate. Check Uniform Commercial Code (UCC) filings with the Secretary of State for other recorded liabilities.

If you are loaning money or buying a note, is the borrower credit worthy? Get a credit report. What is the security for the loan? Is it sufficient? Should you get an appraisal for the property securing the note? Have a lawyer prepare or review the note and security agreement.

Ask for help from a trusted lawyer, CPA or certified financial planner. Better yet, build a team of advisors to help you perform a sanity check.

Lori Greymont, President of SJREI (San Jose Real Estate Investor's Association), allowed me to include her blog post about due diligence, below, in this book. She does coaching for real estate investors, and helps them find prospective investment properties. The web site for SJREI is www.sjrei.org.

> I am often asked what type of "Due Diligence" a person should do before they buy a home. My standard response is "that depends." While it might seem that there should be a standard checklist, there are various elements that affect how much and what type of research on a property you should perform. I come from the background of buying homes for $1,000 - $10,000 off of Bulk REO lists. When I first started investing in these properties, the Due Diligence period was about 5 minutes, so you could only review the list of addresses on a piece of paper and decide if you like the composition of the cities you are investing in.
>
> The pendulum has swung in recent years from banks nearly giving away property to a nationwide inventory shortage. Because of this, the first thing to do before spending any time and money on extensive Due Diligence is to get the desired property into contract. Imagine if you spent five days researching a property only to find out that it went into contract three days ago. This process must first start with control of the property with a contract that allows an appropriate Due Diligence period. This means that you will be able to do your Due Diligence and cancel without any penalty within that time frame if the property isn't what you expected. The length of this period will be determined by your geographical area. Additionally, I know some areas are encouraging offers that don't allow for a Due Diligence period. Don't get caught up in the emotion of bidding to win a property and give this up. Doing so is gambling with your retirement. Your retirement money is not your Las Vegas money! Be smart about this.
>
> Factors that affect how much research on a property you want to complete are the following:

1. How much is the property? Obviously if you are paying $1,000,000 you will want to do more extensive research than if you are paying $5,000.
2. What is the exit plan for the property? If you are going to sell with seller financing, you may not need to do as extensive research as you would if you were going to hold the property for a long period of time.
3. Are you buying it through a traditional method with Title Insurance and a Warranty Deed or through a Quit Claim Deed with all defects? If you are buying it through the traditional method, most all of the liens will be discovered and cleared for you. I say "most" because some utility or compliance liens are not always discovered, so I recommend doing the preliminary work on these as described below. If you are buying the investment with all defects, you will need to be more proactive in your investigation to make sure you know what you are buying.

Evaluate Each Property

The very first step to Due Diligence is to research the market you are investing in. I am not going to spend much time on this today, but your market will affect the performance of your investment and should not be bypassed as unimportant.

Begin by determining a geographical area in which to concentrate. It will be easier to manage your properties in the long run and will help focus your purchasing efforts. Look for neighborhoods that are stable. Use online sources for research as well as conferring with other investors.

Have a team on the ground in that area to visit the property before you buy so you can shorten your Due Diligence time period. You can start building a ground team by calling real estate agents in the area. Interview them for an understanding of the neighborhoods you deal in. Ask for names of handymen they know—you'll need these later and those handymen may become your ground team doing your initial property drive-by assessment. When you are ready to sell, if you need the help of a professional to sell the home, make sure you go back to the people that helped you. Remember that real estate agents only get paid when they sell a house.

Data to Collect for Each Property (and where to find it!)

- MLS.com status: listed price/not listed
- Number of bedrooms, number of bathrooms, square feet
- Type of property (single family home, condo, mobile home)
- www.trulia.com listed price, neighborhood range, number of sales
- Zillow.com listed price
- Date last sold and last sold price
- County assessed value
- Parcel number
- Realestate.yahoo.com price
- FinestExpert.com price
- FinestExpert.com average rent in the area
- **Taxes due (call city + county tax collector)**
- **Water, sewer, garbage, liens, etc. (Do they stay with the house?)**

A Warning About Taxes and Liens

If you are buying a property with a Quit Claim Deed, invest time on the phone calling municipal agencies to uncover back taxes and liens; don't rely on online data only. The information on the internet is a start, but is **notoriously** inaccurate. You must CALL the correct municipal offices. Realize there is a time difference, and that many offices are currently closed on Fridays. Staff is overworked and short tempered. There are long hold times. Be patient, persistent, and be prepared with your parcel number. Beware that if back taxes or liens show nothing owed, that may be because the liens were sold. Ask specific questions like, "If this was left unpaid, would it be sold at some point to someone else?" For example, in some areas of Pennsylvania, the water bill is sold like a tax lien. The bill stays with the house and because of accumulated penalties and interest, can incur tens of thousands of dollars in a short period of time. Plan on calling both the City and the County as they have different jurisdictions. Additional to the Utility Bills that stay with the property, you want to investigate what compliance liens might exist on the property. These liens might occur when the lawn gets mowed by the city or your yard became the neighborhood dumping grounds.

Simple Script You'll have more luck coming across as a gentle concerned homeowner than as an investor. Government employees dislike investors, so be nice. Don't give the rest of us a bad name.
"Hi. This is Jenny Jones. I just bought a house in (city) and I'd like to find out about the current and back (taxes, bills, etc). My address is ________________ (be prepared to provide a parcel or APN number). (Get the info) Thank you. Are there any other city or county offices that I should check with? I really want to make sure I have the entire picture about this property."

Tax and Lien Checklist

- Parcel Number from county assessor
- Amount of County Taxes Owed
- City Taxes Owed
- What Utility Bills stay with the property?
  - Water, Sewer, Garbage, Electric, Gas
- Are any of these owed?
- Existing Code Violations or Fines
- Have tax liens been sold?
- Is property on list for a tax sale?

Property Inspection
After you have determined what is owed, the next part of Due Diligence is to understand the condition of the property. It is best to start out with a general property inspection. Not all states require that property inspectors be licensed or certified, so the quality of the inspection may vary. Also, many property inspectors make their money on the repairs that they identify. It is best to locate a licensed (certified) property inspector who has no ulterior motive for

the inspection except to educate you on the property condition.

Other types of inspections that you may want to order in addition to a general inspection may include a roof, heating and cooling, foundation, and structural and pest inspection. If you are buying in an area that is known for termite infestations, then I would add the pest inspections to the "must" have list of inspections with the property inspection.

Again, all of this comes back to the purpose and cost of the property. Let's say you may be buying a $5,000 property that you plan to sell to another buyer with financing in place. If this is the case, you may only want a property inspection and termite inspection.

On the other hand, let's say you are buying a $500,000 house that you want to renovate and rent out. In that case, it would be worth the money to order the rest of the inspections to mitigate the chance of buying any costly and unforeseen future issues.

Evaluate the Data

The first time you are ready to evaluate all the data you have collected, get experienced assistance. In general, you want to acquire properties where you have room in the price and additional costs to have multiple exit plans for the property should your main plan not work out. Since it is nearly impossible in this current economy to concretely state what a property is worth, you have to do your best by estimating. Talk to others who are investing and selling in your same areas to get a better value comparison and then make your decision.

Lastly, I want to encourage you to not get stuck on trying to recover your research costs and time by forcing the deal to work. If you have done your research, you will know whether the house will work for your planned exit or not. Don't try to force it to work because you want to do a deal. The only way to risk money is to say "Yes," so some of the best money made is on the deals you say "No" to. Many "homeowners" buy on emotion, not logic. Unfortunately, so do many investors. Emotion justifies doing a bad deal when the numbers don't support it. The numbers will either work or they won't. If they don't, quickly move on to your next property. You may lose a little money on the due diligence research, but in the long run, you will earn more money on the profitable deals you do, than the costs on the deals you don't do. Additionally, the amount of time you lose on a deal that won't work can never be recovered. As an investor, if you focus on the numbers and performance of your portfolio of investments over the long run you will be successful.

Some Additional Thoughts on Due Diligence for Real Estate

Craig Martin, CFP® of The Family Wealth Consulting Group offered these additional thoughts about due diligence for real estate investments.

Keep in mind that professional real estate managers are proven experts at performing the best due diligence. They prove that by showing you their track records. Many of the best real estate limited partnerships are managed by general partners with dozens of years of earning much more than most people in this industry and have public track records showing internal rates of return in the mid-teens to low twenties percentages. Of course, this number is reported as an average, so there will be individual investments that greatly outperform while others will significantly underperform the stated average.

That means, if you expect to earn the average, you need to plan to make multiple investments in the same asset class (such as residential real estate or commercial real estate), preferably with competing managers over your lifetime. Finding the most successful people in the category you want to invest in can take as much research as looking at any single address you might buy on your own.

Alternatively, you can hire a certified financial planner who is compensated by fees, not commissions. These advisors work for you, not a large brokerage company. If you choose to manage properties by yourself, then you are choosing to compete with professionals with proven track records who could be working for you. These professionals would always recommend that you create a diversified investment portfolio.

7
What kinds of transactions can you do with your Roth or IRA? (Prohibited transactions.)

When you have a self-directed Roth or IRA account, it can feel like you have a tax-sheltered checkbook. As I discussed in Chapter 5, there is a wide range of choices of possible investments that you can make using these accounts.

The liberalized ability to convert other accounts to Roth accounts is especially exciting, because by meeting fairly liberal requirements, amounts withdrawn from a Roth are tax-free. (Of course there is that small problem of paying the income taxes for a conversion…) Not only that, but you aren't required to take required minimum distributions during your lifetime and, if you have personal service income, you can continue contributing to a Roth even when you are older than age 70 1/2.

In order to have the most choices of investments, you will probably have to use a custodian that is not a traditional bank, brokerage company or mutual fund. Conventional custodians will offer a more restricted menu of choices.

There are three constraints to be concerned about:

1) Roths and IRAs aren't permitted to own some investments, like collectibles and S corporation stock. See Chapter 5.
2) Roths and IRAs can be subject to income taxes on Unrelated Business Taxable Income when debt is used to finance the investment or the investment is deemed to be a trade or business operation. This is not a deal killer, but should be considered when estimating your return on investment for an investment alternative. See Chapter 10.
3) Certain transactions aren't permitted for Roths and IRAs. They are called "prohibited transactions," and can result in disqualification of the account and immediate taxation.

In this chapter, I'm going to focus on prohibited transactions. I am only going to hit some highlights so you will be aware of some red flags. When you are using a self-directed Roth or IRA for alternative investments (investments other than stocks, bonds, savings accounts and mutual funds), you should consult with a team of advisors including an investment advisor, a tax advisor (CPA, enrolled agent, enrolled actuary or tax attorney) and an attorney schooled in retirement accounts. Some self-directed custodians have a directory of professionals familiar with the rules to help you.

As part of its service, a custodian for a self-directed Roth or IRA account should educate its clients about prohibited transactions and watch the activity of its account owners for potential prohibited transactions.

Prohibited transactions are defined primarily at Internal Revenue Code Section 4975.

For IRAs and Roth IRAs, the penalty for a prohibited transaction is disqualification of the account and acceleration of any taxable income.[6] The account is considered to be distributed on the first day of the year during which the prohibited transaction happened. An extreme penalty such as this dictates that the IRA owner must give serious attention to avoiding prohibited transactions. If there are any investments that are sensitive and could result in a prohibited transaction, they should be held in separate IRA or Roth IRA accounts to insulate other retirement assets from exposure to the disqualification penalty.

The penalty for other retirement accounts is a 15% excise tax on the amount involved. If the prohibited transaction isn't timely corrected, an excise tax of 100% of the amount involved can be imposed. The excise tax is reported on Form 5330. You can find the form at www.irs.gov.

Red flags should go up any time there is a transaction between the Roth or IRA and a "party in interest" (also called "disqualified persons"). A party in interest includes a plan fiduciary (custodian or owner), and family members of the account owner including the spouse, descendants (children, grandchildren) and their spouses, and ancestors (parents, grandparents) and their spouses, and entities controlled (50% or more of capital interest or voting power) by a fiduciary or listed family member of the owner or fiduciary. Employees and 10% owners of capital or profits of controlled entities are also parties in interest. However, employees aren't

[6] Internal Revenue Code § 408(e)(2)

disqualified persons unless they are highly compensated, meaning they individually earn 10% or more of the aggregate wages paid by the employer.

I'm not going to discuss this in depth, but here are a few items to be aware of:

The owner of the account can't use or rent a house owned by the account. However, a house can be rented at fair market value to an unrelated person or to a brother or sister of the owner. In the case of renting to a brother or sister, be sure the rent is at fair market rates or you could violate party-in-interest rules or the "exclusive benefit rule."

The owner of the account may not handle cash (currency) for the entity or pay expenses for the entity from a petty cash fund or for reimbursement by the entity.

To avoid accidentally tripping yourself, it's probably best to hire an independent property manager to collect rents and pay expenses of real estate investments.

The owner can't "do the work" to rehabilitate an investment property. (No tearing out sheet rock and hammering new sheet rock yourself!) The owner should find an unrelated independent contractor to do the work.

The Roth or IRA can't make a loan to the owner or a disqualified person, but can make a loan to a brother or sister of the owner, or to any unrelated person or an indirect relative, like an uncle or an aunt. The loan should be handled in a businesslike manner, with a written note and security, and paid promptly. The transaction should not be a disguised gift. Again, when renting to a relative such as a brother or sister, the rent should be at a market rate.

A Roth or IRA can participate in an investment together with a disqualified person, such as forming a new C corporation (not S corporation) or limited liability company (LLC). The rationale for this position is there is no prohibited transaction for setting up the arrangement at inception because the disqualified interest doesn't exist until the entity is formed.[7] You need to be very careful in operating these entities to avoid prohibited transactions after the entity is formed. The entity must be adequately funded to avoid having to make additional capital contributions in the future. It can also be sticky if one of the investors decides to stop participating and has to be bought out!

As an example of an operational disqualification, an IRA was disqualified because the IRA owner, who also owned the majority of an LLC, received wages as general manager of the LLC. The IRA owner received wages of $9,754 in 2005 and $29,263 in 2006. His taxable income from termination of the IRA exceeded $300,000 plus penalties and interest. Don't plan on acquiring a business using your Roth or IRA and drawing a salary from it.[8]

Capital contributions can be made by an IRA to an entity wholly owned by the IRA, such as a single member LLC, without a prohibited transaction problem, due to an exemption for an intra-company transfer.

Capital contributions can also be made to an entity provided the disqualified person doesn't own 50% or more of the entity (including the ownership interests of any other direct relatives, collectively).[9] We are talking about a very delicate subject here. Only proceed with professional guidance.

The Roth or IRA can't buy real estate from a disqualified person.

When the account owner meets requirements such as reaching age 59 1/2, he or she can distribute assets, such as a house, from a Roth account tax-free. So, a strategy to buy a retirement home could be to buy it in a Roth account, rent it to someone other than a disqualified person until it's paid off (subject to unrelated business income tax on the financed part of income), and then distribute it tax-free after retirement.

---

[7] *Swanson v. Commissioner*, 106 T.C. No. 76, February 14, 1996

[8] *Ellis*, 2015-1 U.S.T.C. ¶ 50,328, June 5, 2015

[9] Internal Revenue Code § 4975(e)(2)(G)

Possible "cure" for a prohibited transaction

If you make a "foot fault" and have a prohibited transaction, all may not be lost. You can apply to the Department of Labor for an exemption from the prohibited transaction rules. The exemption can be retroactive. This is an expensive and time consuming process but can be worth it to avoid disqualification of your account.

The Department of Labor has published a procedure to apply for an exemption, RIN 1210-AB49, 2011 ARD 207-1 (October 27, 2011) and regulations (ESBA final regulations, 76 FR 66637, October 27, 2011) explaining the procedure to apply for an exemption. A web page with details is https://www.dol.gov/agencies/ebsa/employers-and-advisers/guidance/exemptions/individual. Get professional help with preparing this application.

8
Making alternative investments in a Roth or IRA using a self-directed account

Many securities brokerage companies and banks offer "self-directed" IRA and Roth accounts. Although these plans do offer some flexibility, they typically offer a menu of choices that doesn't include alternatives like private mortgages, real estate, and non-publicly traded business investments.

You don't need to have a big account to benefit from a self-directed Roth or IRA. For example, an investment that can generate highly leveraged returns is an option to purchase real estate. The option can often be secured by a retirement account with a modest investment. It can possibly be resold to a willing investor for a substantial profit. Since these options are capital assets, the income for reselling the options shouldn't be unrelated business taxable income. Real estate investment training courses explain this approach. Be sure to work with a real estate attorney when you first use it. Using an option has the potential of generating a huge return with a small investment.

Companies have been created that offer custodian services permitting holding these alternative investments.

There is a price to be paid to have this flexibility in the form of higher fees and potentially higher risk.

When choosing one of these custodians, do some investigation or due diligence. (See Chapter 6 for some approaches.) Is the company substantial so that you can rely on it to continue in existence to hold your assets? What safeguards or oversight is it subject to? Is it regulated? Does it have audited financial statements? Does the company provide education or other information about your responsibilities in maintaining a self-directed account? Does the company monitor potential prohibited transactions that could subject the account owner to a penalty or plan disqualification? Is it a member of the Retirement Industry Trust Association (RITA), the association for such regulated custodians?

Some alternative investments can result in taxable income for a Roth or IRA. See Chapter 10, "When IRAs and Roths pay taxes". In most cases, the account owner is responsible for having the tax returns prepared for the IRA or Roth. Since the unrelated business income tax is one of the most complex areas of the Internal Revenue Code, you should probably hire a professional tax return preparer who is familiar with the rules to prepare the income tax returns. This is an additional expense to consider when deciding to use a self-directed IRA and to make an investment subject to the tax versus other alternatives.

The checkbook LLC

Having another operating entity owned by the Roth or IRA can provide three important advantages:

1. Institutions tend to move slowly. You could identify an opportunity, such as buying a foreclosed property on the courthouse steps, but not have access to the cash in time to take advantage of it. If the cash is held in an operating entity, a cashier's check can be immediately generated.

2. Many custodians charge fees for each transaction. If you are paying bills for operating a business or a rental property, you could write hundreds of checks in a year. You can avoid per transaction fees by paying the bills using a checking account for an operating entity.

3. Some investments can involve risks that could impact other assets owned by the Roth or IRA. You can isolate those risks, protecting other assets owned by the Roth or IRA, using a limited liability "envelope," like a corporation or limited liability company. (In addition, you can and probably should set up a separate IRA or Roth account to hold the investment that you wish to isolate.)

Making the decision to form an entity involves important legal issues, so I recommend that you consult with an attorney before going ahead. I also recommend that you use an attorney to form the entity and to monitor its operations to assure you qualify for the liability protection that you are trying to accomplish.

In most cases, the best entity form for the operating entity is a Limited Liability Company (LLC). LLCs can have a manager (the account owner) that is different from the owner (the IRA or Roth). Single-owner LLCs are generally "disregarded entities" for income tax reporting. That means any taxable activities are reported on the income tax return for the IRA or Roth, and any transaction of the single-member LLC is deemed to be a transaction of the IRA or Roth. It also means the LLC itself is generally not subject to income taxes. In contrast, a "regular" or "C" corporation must file its own income tax returns and pay income taxes.

Be aware an LLC can have its own tax or other compliance requirements. In California, a single-member LLC must file an annual report, Form 568. In addition, LLCs registered in California pay an annual $800 tax and those with $250,000 or more of California-source gross receipts pay an annual "fee" of $900 to $11,790 based on the amount of gross receipts. The tax and fee apply even when the LLC has an operating loss! (The California Franchise Tax Board's web site is www.ftb.ca.gov.)

California LLCs must also file a Statement of Information plus a filing fee every two years with the California Secretary of State.

Reporting requirements vary from state to state, so check the requirements for the states your LLC is organized in and the states your LLC operates in. You can do it online, but you can shortcut the process for a fee by using a tax consultant or attorney.

Since a single member LLC is a disregarded entity, it is subject to the same prohibited transaction restrictions as the IRA or Roth. See chapter 7 on prohibited transactions. Avoid expensive litigation with the IRS by avoiding prohibited transactions. An owner-manager should avoid loans and avoid handling currency. It's better to have a property manager collect rent and pay expenses for investment properties.

In some cases, you might want the Roth or IRA to make a joint investment with a "party in interest" or "disqualified person." These investments must be handled with special care. You should assure there is adequate funding when the investment is formed, because additional investments after formation may be prohibited transactions. See chapter 7.

(Advisors don't agree on the desirability of checkbook LLCs. For example, Tom Anderson, President of the Retirement Industry Trust Association (RITA), commented that RITA generally does not favor checkbook LLCs because they tend to be used to deliberately circumvent custodial procedure designed to prevent prohibited transactions or lead unintentionally to prohibited transactions because owners are not familiar with the ever-changing landscape. Some RITA member firms require that owners of single-member IRA-owned LLCs sign a contract agreeing to acquire the services of a qualified professional (CPA or attorney) to review all LLC transactions in advance of execution for compliance with the rules before they will allow the owner to create the LLC with their firm. This requirement enables the IRA owner to take advantage of the benefits of a single-member LLC, while providing extra protection to avoid a violation of the prohibited transaction rules. He believes they will probably be prohibited in the future if the Department of Labor continues to see prohibited transaction violations involving checkbook LLCs.)

Conclusion

The decision to make alternative investments using a self-directed account is an important one. The price is additional expense, complexity, investment risk, and exposure for potential prohibited transactions. When the account owner is operating in an area that he or she understands or with the assistance of a skilled investment advisor, CPA or attorney and can generate significantly greater returns, plus get greater investment diversification in the process, using a self-directed IRA or Roth, possibly together with a checkbook LLC, can make sense.

9
A case study

Dick Blakeley, CEO of The Blakeley Group, Inc., a registered investment advisor firm, volunteered to provide this case study/example of an actual client situation where a self-directed IRA was used to accomplish a client's financial goals. The web site for The Blakeley Group, Inc. is www.theblakeleygroup.com.

Scenario: A small manufacturing and distribution company is doing a business of several millions of dollars in sales. It is slightly profitable and has positive cash flow. The company has about $500,000 in accounts receivable and $500,000 in inventory. The cash flow for the company is tight because of new orders. The company could obtain volume discounts based on the size of the orders. Previously, the company had borrowed just enough funds, through a factoring company, to keep inventory on the shelf. To add to the challenge, one of the companies that had financed inventory had filed for Chapter 11 Bankruptcy.

Another problem the company has is the factoring company charges about 24% per year and is costing the company a significant amount of its pre-tax earnings and many small banks do not lend to this type of company. The company at any one time has about $600,000 in receivables being factored and the cost is about $144,000 per month in cash flow. The company realizes if it could bring down the interest it pays for factoring: a) the cash flow would more than double and b) the company could more than triple its earnings.

The owners of the company have friends and family who have IRAs and retirement plans with big balances and who are earning less than 4% interest on the funds deposited in their plans. In addition, they believe those same friends and family members would be willing to invest part of their funds in a fixed income note secured with the inventory and receivables in the company if only there was a way to make such an investment.

The owners of the company had an "Aha!" moment and come up with a winning solution for both the company and their friends who have low earning IRAs. The company owners spoke with their friends to see how many would truly like to participate in such a note and they got great feedback on the idea. They worked with their CPA and their attorney and found out there was an opportunity to create a Limited Liability Company (LLC) as a lending facility.

The LLC would be owned by IRAs and individuals and could be managed by the owners of the IRAs and the individual investors. (Note that owners of the company and some of their relatives, including their IRAs, can't participate to avoid a prohibited transaction. The ownership structure of the LLC should be reviewed by an attorney to assure the prohibited transaction rules aren't violated. Also, an individual who is an owner of an IRA usually shouldn't invest in the same LLC as their IRA.) The LLC would make agreements with the company to lend capital to the company at better rates than the factoring company. In return the LLC would receive monthly cash from the company and the LLC would be the lien holder on the receivables and the inventory. The LLC would be listed as one of the beneficiaries on a key-man policy and the company has E&O insurance to cover the principals of the company.

An LLC was formed to receive funds from IRAs and individuals to lend to the manufacturing company. In return for the loans, the LLC held a security interest in the inventory and the receivables. Contracts are made with the manufacturing company with terms to include the interest to be paid, the collateral being secured, an agreement accounting for the collateral and the aging of receivables, the rate of discount to be used so there will be a margin of safety for the investors, and an agreement that the company will pay all accounting, legal, and professional fees.

The LLC managers have an independent party receive the monthly cash flow, pay taxes, prepare taxes, pay the investors, and bi-annually verify the collateral owned by the company but secured by the LLC and send out periodic letters to the note holders updating on their work and observation on the accounts receivables and inventory.

The loan documents contain an important clause which will allow for substitution of collateral by the company. This is important because the inventory is turning over through the company and the LLC filed a Uniform Commercial Code (UCC) with the state and county to codify the terms of the loan between the company and the LLC and notify all other potential lenders that the terms of the loan needed to be satisfied and the collateral be released before another lender could use the collateral for another loan.

Here are some key points:

- The interest rate needs to follow state law guidelines as to the maximum interest it can collect and pay (anti-usury rules). If the rates are above the rate given in the guidelines, the LLC will need to apply for a special lending license.
- Investors like and need to be kept informed on the issues around the loans.
- The investors need to fully accept that there is and will be no liquid market for the loan and, as a result, they need to agree to the reality that they may need to hold onto the loan until the note matures.
- In this kind of a private transaction, the LLC needs its own independent counsel/attorney to represent the LLC.
- The LLC's attorney needs to prepare documentation for the investors to verify that they have the means and the sophistication to invest in the private note.
- The LLC's attorney needs to prepare and see the loan documents with the company fully executed, including the UCC filings.

End Result...

The company replaced its high-priced debt with a five year note for which it pays 10% to private investors using part of the investors' retirement funds. The private investors received significantly higher interest rates than they would have received from their banks or credit unions and the investors felt comfortable because their investment in the LLC's note was collateralized. Both sides benefited from the other's needs.

Epilogue...

The company paid interest as agreed for more than four of the loan's five year term and the owner died in a car crash. The loan was fully repaid with the proceeds from the key man's life insurance policy and the owner's spouse sold the company to its employees.

Notes from Michael Gray –

Private loans can be good investments for self-directed IRAs, because interest income isn't subject to tax to the IRA or Roth as unrelated business taxable income. In Dick's case study, the interest rate is attractive and the note is secured with accounts receivable and inventory. You still need to be careful to avoid loans to certain related parties (including companies owned by certain family members), which can be prohibited transactions. I would prefer to have the management of the LLC be independent of the management of the company that is borrowing the funds. See the chapters on those subjects.

10
When Roths and IRAs owe income taxes – The Unrelated Business Income Tax

Many people aren't aware that "tax exempt" entities, including charities and retirement plans, are subject to income taxes on certain types of income, called "unrelated business taxable income." How to apply the tax rules for unrelated business taxable income is one of the more complex areas of the income tax laws.

Just because an activity owned by a Roth or IRA is subject to unrelated business income tax doesn't mean you shouldn't do it. The key issues are: 1) What is the net return on investment after income taxes and compliance costs? and 2) What is the risk to get that return? If the return is greater than your other alternatives with a reasonable risk, it can be favorable to go ahead with the activity. With banks paying very low interest for certificates of deposit and a volatile stock market, many people will find it hard to keep up with inflation without making alternative investments.

The federal tax form on which the income tax is computed for tax-exempt entities is Form 990-T, Exempt Organization Income Tax Return. You can get a copy of the form and instructions at the IRS web site, www.irs.gov.

When tax-exempt trusts, like retirement accounts, are subject to the tax on unrelated business income, they are generally taxed under the rules and rates that apply to trusts. The first $1,000 of unrelated business income is not subject to tax. For 2018, taxable income over $12,500 is subject to the 37% maximum federal income tax rate.

For example, when many real estate properties are bought and sold during a tax year in "quick turn" transactions, these transactions may be determined to be a trade or business. ("Occasional" sales of properties, especially without rehabilitation, is not a trade or business. The crossover point from "investor" to "dealer" hasn't been clearly defined.) The properties are not considered to be held for investment, but for sale to customers in the ordinary course of a trade or business. These transactions and related business expenses should be reported as unrelated business income.

The IRS has "looked through" an IRA to find a "wash sale" for a sale of securities by the participant and purchase by the IRA. For many purposes, the IRS treats multiple IRA accounts as one account, such as when computing required minimum distributions. This may be an indication the IRS could try to aggregate "quick sale" transactions in multiple IRA accounts to find a trade or business, resulting in unrelated business income.

Another type of activity that is probably a business is subdividing land and building homes for resale.

There is a special exception for property purchased by a tax exempt entity from a financial institution in conservatorship or receivership or from the conservator or receiver of such a financial institution. The property must have been identified within the 9-month period beginning on the date of its acquisition as property held for sale, but no more than one-half of property acquired in a single transaction may be designated. The sale must take place before the later of (1) the date 30 months after the date of acquisition of the property, or (2) a date otherwise specified by the IRS. While the property was held by the tax exempt entity, the total expenditures on improvements and development activities included in the basis of the property may not exceed 20% of the net selling price of the property.

Trade or business income of a partnership or an S corporation for which the tax-exempt entity has an ownership interest is unrelated business income. There is a special exception for S corporation employer shares held by an Employee Stock Ownership Plan (ESOP). IRAs and Roths aren't permitted shareholders for S corporations anyway.

Any income received from a "controlled entity," including rental income which would usually not be subject to tax, is taxed as net unrelated trade or business income.

Generally, rental income from rental real estate is not unrelated business income, but see below about debt-financed income. Rent from personal property that is incidental to renting real estate is also not unrelated business income. To be "incidental," the rent for the personal property may not exceed 10% of the total rents for all property leased.

Gains from the sale of real estate are also generally not unrelated business income, unless the property is inventory or held for sale to customers for a trade or business, or the gain is debt-financed income.

Unrelated debt-financed income

Real estate is an especially attractive investment vehicle because you can use leverage to enhance your returns. This means you can finance a big portion of the purchase price and control a big value of property with a relatively small cash investment.

When you use leverage to purchase property in an IRA or Roth, a proportionate part of the income, including rental income and gain when the property is sold, is unrelated business taxable income. A percentage (an average of the acquisition indebtedness divided by the average adjusted basis of the property during the period it's held by the organization during the taxable year) is applied to the income and deductions to compute the amounts to be reported on the unrelated business tax return.

There is a special exception from the unrelated debt-financed income rule for company retirement accounts, such as 401(k)s (including single-person or solo 401(k)s) , profit-sharing plans and pension plans (but not Simplified Employee Pensions (SEPs)) and government retirement accounts. The fact that you can make leveraged investments in real estate that are exempt from the unrelated business income tax makes company retirement accounts very attractive compared to IRAs or Roths, which are not exempt when they engage in leveraged transactions.

Since the custodian firms for self-directed IRA accounts typically don't prepare the tax forms for unrelated business income tax and the tax is complex, you should consider having the tax return for unrelated business tax prepared by a professional tax return preparation firm who is familiar with the tax.

11
Where to get help with your investments

After the stock market decline during 2008, a common "joke" was the "201(k) account." Many people found they had to postpone their retirements or return to work.

Those who were able to "ride out the storm" and stayed invested experienced a historic market recovery. Their investments have substantially recovered.

Where can you get investment advice to guide you during turbulent times, including information about alternative investments?

A resource to consider in most communities is the fee-only Certified Financial Planner (CFP®). These individuals have received considerable education relating to investing and personal financial management. They have learned to deal with a client's total financial picture. Since their income is solely based on fees, they don't have a financial interest in the investment decisions of their clients and can provide independent advice.

I suggest that you watch my television interviews with financial planner Craig Martin, CFP® entitled "Investing In Turbulent Times" and "The Role of the Fee-Only Financial Planner" at my web site, www.financialinsiderweekly.com. (By the way, this television series was strictly educational and a great source of financial education. I discontinued producing the show late in 2017, but most of the interviews are still relevant.)

There are also community education groups where you can get information. Such a group in Silicon Valley is the San Jose Real Estate Investors Association. You can get information about their meetings at www.sjrei.org.

Learn to distinguish gambling and speculation (short-term, high-risk trades) versus investing (long-term).

Study investment books to make more informed decisions. A classic book on securities investing is *A Random Walk Down Wall Street.* Other books to look at are *Craig Martin on Asset Class Investing* (call 408-453-2224 for a copy) and Nick Murray's book, *Simple Wealth, Inevitable Wealth.*

12
Creating a bigger account – rollovers from qualified plans (401(k)s)

When advisors suggest considering investing in alternative investments in a Roth or IRA account, people often object, "I don't have very much available in my Roth or IRA to invest!"

The advisor may then ask, "Do you have a 401(k) or other retirement plan at work?"

"Yes, I have a 401(k) account with about $100,000 in it."

It may be that the $100,000 401(k) balance can be rolled over to a Roth or IRA account. (Of course the rollover to a Roth could be taxable. See Chapter 13. If the 401(k) account was a Roth 401(k) account, the rollover generally wouldn't be taxable.)

New fiduciary rules make it harder for financial advisors to recommend rollovers. It's easier for them if the account owner simply requests a rollover.

Pension portability has been tremendously increased by the Economic Growth and Tax Relief Act of 2001 and the Pension Protection Act of 2006. With a few limitations, funds can be rolled over from employer retirement accounts to a Roth or IRA account and, in some cases, from a Roth or IRA account to an employer retirement account. We used to be concerned with segregating rollover funds from qualified plans for future rollovers to other qualified plans. This is no longer a concern. Even partial rollovers are permitted and you don't have to be more than age 59 1/2 to qualify if the distribution is made as a direct "trustee to trustee" transfer.

Not all employer plans permit such an "in service" transfer, so that can be an issue. Perhaps the employer can be persuaded to amend the plan to permit such transfers.

Before September 18, 2014, the only way to transfer non-deductible employee contributions from an employer plan to a Roth or IRA was through a direct "trustee to trustee" transfer.

On or after September 18, 2014, any pretax (taxable) employee contributions from an employer plan are first allocated to direct "trustee to trustee" transfers. Any pretax amounts in excess of direct transfers are next allocated according to the participant's selection of plans that receive 60-day rollovers. Any remaining pretax amounts are allocated to cash received and are taxable income. In order to qualify for this treatment, the recipient plan must agree to separately account for after-tax contributions. [10]

When making the above allocations, the pretax amounts are computed using a ratio of the pretax contributions to the total value of the account before the distribution. For example, Jane Employee elects to distribute $100,000 from a 401(k) account with a $250,000 balance and to which Jane made $50,000 of nondeductible contributions. The pretax portion of the distribution is $200,000 / $250,000 = 80% X $100,000 = $80,000.

If Jane received the $100,000 distribution in cash and elected to rollover $80,000 to a regular IRA and $20,000 to a Roth account within 60 days of receiving the distribution, Jane can designate the after tax amount would be allocated to the $20,000 rollover amount to the Roth account so there would be no taxable income from the Roth conversion, and $80,000 pretax amount would be allocated to the regular IRA for a continued tax deferral.

Work with the employer and Roth or IRA custodian to timely complete any paperwork required to designate where the pretax amount is being allocated.

Required minimum distributions and hardship distributions can't be rolled over from an employer plan to a Roth or IRA.

The advantage of having the funds in a Roth or IRA account is to have the ability to make alternative investments for more diversification,

---

[10] Notice 2014-54, September 18, 2014, REG-105739-11, September 18, 2014

such as investing in pre-IPO stock, real estate, and private money mortgages. (See Chapter 5.)

The disadvantage of having the funds in a Roth or IRA account is the assets might have less bankruptcy protection, particularly if the funds were contributed and were not rollovers from 401(k) or other qualified employer retirement accounts. Employer plans have superior asset protection. Consult with a lawyer about this before going ahead with a transfer from an employer retirement account to a Roth or IRA. It may be you should be transferring assets to the employer plan instead of the Roth or IRA!

What about inherited employer accounts? After 2009, beneficiaries must be permitted to rollover the balance to a beneficiary Roth or IRA account. The IRS surprised tax advisors by explaining that rules adopted by Congress permit a direct transfer of an inherited employer retirement account to a Roth account in Notice 2008-30. Inherited IRA accounts can't be converted to Roth accounts.[11] (Again, such a transfer would be subject to income tax.)

So, open your mind. You might have more investment flexibility with your retirement funds than you thought. Also, always seek competent professional advice when making such large financial decisions.

[11] Internal Revenue Code Section 408(d)(3)(C)

13

Converting a tax deferred account to a tax-free account – at a price (Roth conversions)

Starting in 2010, the ability to convert an IRA to a Roth IRA was dramatically liberalized, enabling many individuals who couldn't have a Roth IRA before to have one. The rules were also extended to enable the conversion of a "regular" 401(k) account to a Roth 401(k) account. (The 401(k) plan must offer a "Roth" feature to make such a conversion.)

Previously, such a conversion wasn't allowed if your modified adjusted gross income was more than $100,000. This restriction has been eliminated.

The "price" for the conversion is the amount converted is taxable as ordinary income. The conversion is reported on Form 8606, "Nondeductible IRAs." The penalty for distributions before age 59 ½ does not apply to Roth conversions. The penalty can apply when a distribution is made from the Roth account before age 59 ½ and within five years after the conversion.

Direct conversions from qualified plan accounts (such as a 401(k) or profit sharing account) to Roth IRA accounts are also permitted. The plan must permit "in-service" distributions in order to make a conversion before retirement or separation from service.

A named beneficiary of an inherited qualified plan account may also make a direct conversion to a Roth account. Avoid an "intermediary" transfer of an inherited employer plan account to a regular IRA, because that will disqualify the conversion. Conversions of inherited regular IRAs to Roth IRAs aren't permitted.

Here are two reasons for considering converting a regular IRA or retirement account balance to a Roth during 2018:

1. **<u>The Medicare (net investment income) tax.</u>** An additional 3.8% tax on net investment income, including most taxable long-term capital gains, became effective in 2013. The tax

applies for individuals with modified adjusted gross income exceeding $200,000 for singles, $250,000 for married persons filing joint returns, and $125,000 for married persons filing separate returns.

This tax does not apply to distributions from retirement accounts, but will apply to earnings from reinvested distributions. There are no required distributions for a Roth IRA account during the original owner's lifetime.

Taxable distributions from regular IRAs could increase a taxpayer's adjusted gross income, subjecting investment income to the net investment income tax.

2. **Tax-free accumulation of earnings.** After a short waiting period, most earnings in Roth IRAs are income tax-free while accumulated in the account and when distributed. (There is an exception for unrelated business taxable income in the Roth account. It won't apply to most taxpayers. See Chapter 10.) There is a toll to pay, since the Roth conversion is taxable.

   The younger the account owner, the bigger the advantage of this tax-free accumulation. Since an inherited account can be distributed over the beneficiary's life expectancy, this avoidance can continue for a long time after the original account owner is deceased. The younger the beneficiary, the bigger the advantage, provided the beneficiary doesn't accelerate distributions.

Effective 2018, you can no longer change your mind

For tax years beginning before 2018, if a Roth conversion of a regular IRA was made during a taxable year, it could be reversed by a trustee-to-trustee transfer to a regular IRA no later than the extended due date of the federal tax return for the year. The accumulated earnings attributable to the conversion amount were also required to be transferred to the regular IRA account to qualify as a reversal. (Note this election is still available for 2017 income tax returns.

The Tax Cuts and Jobs Act repealed this election for tax years beginning after December 31, 2017. Once you have made a Roth conversion, you can't "undo" it. (Note that contributions other than conversions to an IRA or a Roth can still be recharacterized up to the extended due date of an income tax return.)

You ***can't*** change your mind when you convert a 401(k) account or 457 plan account to a Roth 401(k) or 457 account.

Using a conversion to beat Roth contribution limits

For 2018, annual Roth contributions (other than rollovers and conversions) are phased out for "modified adjusted gross income" from \$118,000 to \$133,000 for singles, \$180,000 to \$199,000 for married persons filing joint returns, and \$0 to \$10,000 for married persons filing separate returns.

If you have no IRA accounts for previous years, you can make a \$5,500 non-deductible IRA contribution for 2017 up to April 17, 2018. The non-deductible IRA can then be converted to a Roth account. There may be little or no taxable income for income accumulated in the non-deductible IRA after setting it up. Effectively, the Roth contribution limits are defeated in this scenario. (Michael Jones, CPA believes there is a risk the IRS could use the step-transaction theory to disallow this tactic.)

If you already have "regular" IRA accounts accumulated through funding with deductible contributions in prior years and/or with rollovers from qualified plans, such as 401(k) accounts, all of the IRA accounts are treated as one account when a distribution is made. This means a Roth conversion after a non-deductible contribution to a "regular" IRA will carry out taxable income attributable to deductible contributions and rollovers from all of the taxable IRA accounts.

For example, if a regular IRA previously only had tax deductible contributions and had an opening balance of \$45,000, and a \$5,000 non-deductible contribution was made for 2017, followed by a \$5,000 Roth conversion, the taxable income for the conversion would be \$4,500. (\$5,000 X \$45,000 / \$50,000.)

Conclusion

Now that regular IRA and retirement accounts can be converted to Roths regardless of the level of income, taxpayers have considerably more flexibility to accumulate more funds in Roth accounts. These transactions should be made under the guidance of a tax advisor who is familiar with the rules, together with a financial advisor.

14
What distributions can you take from a Roth or IRA before age 59 ½?

Individual retirement accounts

Distributions from an individual retirement account before the participant reaches age 59 ½ are subject to a 10% federal additional penalty income tax. (California has a 2.5% penalty tax.)

The 10% penalty tax doesn't apply to the following partial list of distributions:

1. Distributions made on or after the date on which the IRA owner attains age 59 ½.

2. Distributions made due to the IRA owner's death or disability.

3. Distributions that are part of a series of substantially equal periodic payments made for the IRA owner's life or the joint lives of the IRA owner and his or her beneficiary. (See below.)

4. Distributions for medical expenses in excess of the 7 ½% (for 2017 and 2018, scheduled to increase to 10% thereafter) of adjusted gross income floor.

5. Distributions used to pay health insurance premiums to an individual after separation from employment.

6. Distributions used to pay "qualified higher education expenses" of the participant, the participant's spouse, or any child or grandchild of the participant or the participant's spouse.

7. Distributions used to pay certain expenses incurred by qualified first-time homebuyers (explained below).

8. Distributions due to an IRS levy on the IRA.

9. Qualified hurricane and disaster distributions (cumulative $100,000 limit).

10. Distributions to individuals called to active military duty for more than 179 days after September 11, 2001.

Substantially equal periodic payments

Payments can be made based on the IRS life expectancy tables used to compute required minimum distributions, recomputed annually. (See Chapter 16.)

This election can be made by individuals who need access to their IRA funds before age 59 ½ and who want to avoid penalties.

Although in most cases all IRA accounts are aggregated, this election can be made on an account-by-account basis.

Once the election has been made, the payments must continue annually until the later of the date the participant reaches age 59 ½ or five years have elapsed.

Qualified first-time homebuyer distributions

"Qualified first-time homebuyer distributions" are withdrawals from an IRA or Roth IRA of up to $10,000 during the participant's lifetime that are used within 120 days of withdrawal to buy, build, or rebuild a principal residence of the participant, spouse, child, or grandchild of the participant or the participant's spouse. In order to be a first-time homebuyer, the individual and the individual's spouse, if married, must not have had an ownership interest in a principal residence during a two-year period ending on the date the new home is acquired.

Roth distributions

Qualified distributions from a Roth IRA are not included in the taxpayer's gross income and are not subject to the 10% federal early withdrawal tax.

To be a qualified distribution, the distribution must satisfy a five-year holding period and meet one of the following additional requirements:

1. Made on or after the date on which the participant is age 59 ½.

2. Distribution on or after the participant's death.

3. Distribution for disability.

4. Distribution used to pay for "qualified first-time homebuyer expenses" (same as for IRAs, above.)

To meet the five-year holding period, the distribution may not be made before the end of the five-tax-year period beginning with the first tax year for which the individual (or the individual's spouse) made a contribution to the Roth IRA.

There is also a special holding period rule when there was a Roth conversion. See Chapter 13.

A distribution that isn't a qualified distribution may be taxable under an ordering rule. Distributions are first from contributions, so distributions aren't taxable until the total amount of contributions is distributed.

Taxable distributions may be subject to the 10% federal early withdrawal tax unless they meet one of the exceptions described above for individual retirement accounts.

Spousal rollover accounts after a death

Note that a surviving spouse who converts an account inherited from his or her deceased spouse to or rolls it over to his or her own account, not as a "beneficiary," is also subject to the above early distribution penalty and also must generally wait until age 59 ½ to avoid the early distribution penalty. See Chapter 19 for more details.

15
Distributions permitted from a Roth or IRA starting age 59 ½ and before age 70 ½

Once the participant reaches age 59 ½ until the participant reaches age 70 ½, the participant has total flexibility for taking distributions from an IRA or Roth (assuming the Roth account has been open at least five years). Distributions are permitted, but not required. (No required minimum distributions are required for a Roth during the participant's lifetime. See Chapter 16.)

There is a special holding period rule when there was a Roth conversion. See Chapter 13.

16
Required annual distributions
during the participant's lifetime after age 70 ½

Once the participant (account owner) reaches age 70 ½, distributions are required to be made annually from regular IRA accounts.

There are no required minimum distributions for a Roth account during the lifetime of the participant/original owner. (Roth 401(k) accounts do have required minimum distributions. This is a reason for rolling a Roth 401(k) account to a Roth IRA account upon retirement.) Beneficiaries who inherit a Roth IRA account do have required minimum distributions. See the Chapter 19 on handling IRA and Roth accounts after a death.

When an IRA or Roth is annuitized, it is handled separately from other IRAs. Distributions are made according to an annuity schedule that will be handled by the insurance company. DO NOT INCLUDE ANNUITIZED ACCOUNTS WHEN COMPUTING REQUIRED MINIMUM DISTRIBUITONS FOR IRA ACCOUNTS THAT ARE NOT ANNUITIZED. (Most aren't annuitized.)

The IRS has issued regulations relating to computing required minimum distributions when an IRA includes annuitized benefits and non-annuitized benefits.[12] In most cases, it's much simpler to just have separate accounts for each.

The IRS has also issued final regulations excluding "Qualified Longevity Annuity Contracts" purchased on or after July 2, 2014 from the annual required distribution computation. These contracts provide life annuity payments beginning at an advanced age (no later than the first day of the month following the 85th birthday of the participant). The purpose is to help participants hedge the risk of drawing down their benefits too quickly and outliving their retirement savings. The amount permitted to be invested in such contracts is limited to the lesser of $125,000 or 25% of the participant's account balance on the date of the payment.[13] This is a

---

[12] Treasury Regulations § 1.401(a)(9)-8, A-2(a)(3)
[13] T.D. 9673, July 1, 2014

"foot in the door" favoring the insurance industry for at least a portion of retirement accounts.

The initial required minimum distribution is required to be made by April 1 of the year following the year the participant reaches age 70 ½. This means there will be two distributions in the year following the year the participant reaches age 70 ½ (unless the initial required minimum distribution was withdrawn in the year when age 70 ½ was attained).

The distribution is usually computed by dividing the account balance at the end of the previous year by an applicable distribution period from the Uniform Lifetime Table. (The table is included in Appendix B at the end of this book.) You look up the period based on the participant's age at the end of the year. For example, if Jane will be age 71 at the end of 2018 and her account balance was $265,000 at the end of 2017, her required distribution for 2018 will be $265,000 / 26.5 = $10,000.

Notice that the applicable distribution period factor is not reduced by one each year. There is a recalculation based on life expectancy, which is extended for each year the participant survives.

The table includes an extended life expectancy for an assumed beneficiary who is ten years younger than the participant, even if the account has no named beneficiary.

There is an exception when the sole beneficiary of the IRA account is the spouse of the participant and the spouse is more than ten years younger than the participant. There is a special Joint and Last Survivor Table used to determine the applicable distribution period in that case, which you can find in Publication 590B. The calculation process is similar, except you use the factor from the other table, using the ages for both spouses. The standard dual-life table is used even if a charity is named as the primary beneficiary of the account.

Under the required minimum distribution rules, all of the participant's IRA accounts held as the *owner* are treated as one. (Inherited IRA accounts are handled separately. See the chapter on handling IRA and Roth accounts after a death.) The required distribution is computed based on the total account balances (excluding annuitized amounts) at the end of the previous year. The distribution can be withdrawn from one or a combination of accounts.

When computing the account balance as of the end of the previous year, you must increase the balance for any IRA rollovers that haven't been completed by the year-end.[14]

The account balance is not reduced for a required minimum distribution for the year the participant reached age 70 ½ that is paid the next year. (This is a minor disadvantage of postponing payment until the next year.)

[14] Treasury Regulations § 1.401(a)(9)-7, A-2

17
Valuation and retirement accounts

As in many areas of taxation, valuation is a key issue for retirement accounts. However, there is surprisingly little guidance about how valuation should be applied, so valuation is a neglected issue and can be viewed as "the elephant in the room" that few people talk about.

Required minimum distributions are computed based on the "account balance at the beginning of the year".[15] Evidently, the author of the regulations was thinking of retirement accounts like a bank account - a nice, simple cash figure. IRS Publications 590A and 590B on IRAs also describes the IRA account balance as "the amount in the IRA at the end of the year preceding the year for which the required minimum distribution is being figured".

IRAs and Roth custodians are required to report the account balance as of the end of the year at line 5 of Form 5498 so the account owner can compute the required minimum distribution for a taxable year.

Most retirement plan administrators will annually revalue assets that are easy to value, such as marketable securities, certificates of deposit and bank accounts. In the past, they have typically used the cost of hard to value assets, such as partnership interests or corporate stock that isn't publicly traded, when computing the "fair market value" or "account balance." In addition, accrued but unpaid dividends and interest are disregarded for computing the account balance. This is a practical convenience.

The IRS has awakened to this issue. Effective for 2015, the IRS is requiring separate disclosure of the fair market value of specified assets, including stock of corporations that aren't publicly traded, partnership and LLC interests that aren't publicly traded, private mortgages, real estate, non-traded options, and other assets that don't have a readily available fair market value.[16] This information is reported at boxes 15a and 15b of Form 5498. The instructions for Form 5498 simply state that the fair

---

[15] Treasury Regulations § 1.401(a)(9)-5, A-3

[16] 2015 Instructions for Forms 1099-R and 5498, pages 20 and 22

market value is required to be disclosed with no explanation about how it should be determined.

"Fair market value" (FMV) is a loaded description for tax reporting. It represents the amount an informed buyer would pay an informed seller. How you compute FMV has grown into a huge industry, involving "valuation adjustments" for lack of marketability and/or minority interests. Having a business valuation study done for business interests that aren't publicly traded costs thousands of dollars. An appraisal may only be a starting point for determining the fair market value. There may be additional accruals to be considered. Volumes have been written about fair market value. A detailed discussion is beyond the scope of this book.

Rules for computing the value for annuity contracts held inside a defined contribution plan for required minimum distribution purposes are explained at Treasury Regulations § 1.401(a)(9)-6, A-12(a). The details are beyond the scope of this discussion. The method may not be used to value a contract for a Roth IRA conversion. See Treasury Regulations § 1.408A-4, A-14 for annuity contracts distributed in Roth conversions.

If an account balance is understated, the required minimum distribution could be understated, potentially exposing the account owner to a 50% penalty. In addition to required payments after reaching age 70 ½, penalties can apply for a series of substantially equal payments before age 59 ½ and for inherited retirement accounts. (The taxpayer could argue for a "reasonable cause" waiver of penalties. Any formal change in the regulations would likely only apply to future years.)

In the years when no distributions are made or required to be made and there is no Roth conversion, the FMV has no tax consequence. The IRS hasn't stated any consequences of misstating the FMV on Form 5498 in this scenario.

The value on box 5 of Form 5498 can't be used for estate tax reporting. The underlying assets must be valued for that purpose.[17] However, the instructions for Form 5498 now give the plan custodian the option of reporting the date of death or the year-end value for the account

---

[17] Treasury Regulations § 20.2031(b)(1)

on Form 5498 issued to the decedent. According to the instructions, the year-end value will probably be zero because a Form 5498 should be issued to the beneficiary(ies) of the account with the year-end balance(s).

As I understand it, custodians of self-directed Roth and IRA accounts rely on the account owner or the asset sponsor of the investment to provide the fair market value amounts that they report on Form 5498, which are needed from many non-traditional investments. The account owner is responsible for obtaining and paying for any required appraisals. The cost for getting an appraisal of most residential real estate isn't very great, but the cost to appraise a business or other real estate may be prohibitive and lead to the decision to avoid many alternative investments.

18
Estate Planning for IRAs and Roths

The details of estate planning are beyond the scope of this book. You should seek the help of a qualified team of professionals, including an attorney, life insurance agent, tax advisor, financial planner and others.

With the Tax Cuts and Jobs Act of 2017, estate planning has become more uncertain.

The estate and gift tax exemption has been doubled from $5 million to $10 million, indexed for inflation after 2010, effective for tax years beginning after 2017 and expiring for tax years after 2025. The exemption equivalent for 2018 is $11,180,000. Under the current federal estate tax laws, the estate tax exemption is "portable" for surviving spouses. This means the unused exemption for the last-deceased spouse can be available for the surviving spouse, enabling a married couple to have a combined taxable estate of up to $22,360,000 and not be subject to estate tax.

Since the exemption increase expires after 2025, we don't know for certain what will happen after 2025 to exemptions increased using portability elections made by estates of decedents who died before 2026. Congress has directed the IRS to issue regulations to "carry out the purposes of the [portability elections] with respect to differences between the basic exclusion amount in effect: (1) at the time of the decedent's death; and (2) at the time of any gifts made by the decedent." Will the exemption that has increased because of a portability election when a spouse died from 2018 to 2025 but that wasn't used before 2026 be adjusted downward after 2025? We don't know. We have never had the threshold for the lifetime exemption decrease before. Consult with your estate planning attorney about this when making your estate plan. Hopefully the IRS will issue some guidance.

For individuals with estates well below the higher exemptions, the emphasis of estate planning has shifted from estate and gift taxes to income taxes. Trusts are now subject to the maximum federal income tax rate of 37% when their taxable income exceeds $12,500. The 3.8% net investment income tax, in addition to the federal income tax, also applies for trusts when their income exceeds $12,500.

The tax basis of certain assets (excluding retirement accounts, which are considered "income with respect of a decedent") that are included in the taxable estate of a decedent is adjusted to fair market value on the date of death, sometimes called a "stepped-up basis," although it could also be "stepped down." Estate plans are being designed to avoid "bypass" strategies and include appreciated family assets in modest estates, including the use of qualified terminable interest property (QTIP) trusts.

In addition, the various states have different inheritance tax regimes and differences in their laws for transferring property that will require attention from a local attorney.

For most individuals, their retirement accounts represent a major asset. The two major asset classes for most people are their home and their retirement accounts.

On the other hand, retirement accounts are somewhat "invisible" because we don't have regular access to them. They are sometimes neglected in estate planning – a huge mistake.

Here are some estate planning tips for a Roth IRA or regular IRA.

Do wills or trusts govern disposition of the account?

IRAs and Roths are contractual accounts, which means their disposition isn't controlled by a will or trust, but by beneficiary designations by the account owner. An estate or trust can be named as a beneficiary, but this should be done carefully or the tax deferral for the account can be lost.

Generally, an estate should never be named as the beneficiary for an IRA or Roth. A trust under a will, called a testamentary trust, or a stand-alone trust are better alternatives.

A will or trust will control the disposition of the account if the estate or trust is the beneficiary of the account. There are a host of consequences of making an estate or trust the beneficiary, some of which are discussed in this chapter and Chapter 19. Making an estate or trust the beneficiary should not be done lightly, and then only with the counsel of a qualified lawyer and a qualified tax advisor.

Note that if a beneficiary form isn't in effect (hasn't been signed and submitted), the plan document or IRA adoption agreement will specify who the beneficiary will be. For qualified plans, the beneficiary will typically be the surviving spouse. For IRAs, the beneficiary will typically be the estate. As part of the estate planning process, study the plan document.

ERISA joint and survivor annuity requirements

Employer IRA plans other than single employer plans must provide that the benefit will be a qualified joint and survivor annuity. This requirement can be waived. Seek legal counsel if a waiver is desired.

Community property

In community property states, the account owner's spouse may have enforceable rights in the account. If the participant is married and the beneficiary is someone other than the participant's spouse, the spouse may be entitled to compensation when the account goes to the named beneficiary. Consult with legal counsel about the rights of each spouse.

Therefore, a married participant/account owner should get the written consent of his or her spouse, including a valid community property transmutation agreement, if a beneficiary other than the spouse is named. A valid and enforceable transmutation agreement should be prepared with legal guidance. The beneficiary designation must conform with the transmutation agreement. If the participant doesn't get written consent from his or her spouse when the spouse isn't named as the beneficiary, the spouse should get legal advice about how to deal with the situation.

Spouse as sole beneficiary

In most cases, you can get the maximum deferral for the account and achieve the maximum flexibility by naming your spouse as the sole beneficiary. The reason is the surviving spouse has the option of converting the account to his or her own. Most beneficiaries have to compute required distributions using a single life table. Surviving spouses who convert or roll inherited IRAs to their own accounts can compute required distributions using the Uniform Table, based on a joint life expectancy with an assumed beneficiary who is 10 years younger. (But surviving spouses who are less than age 59 ½ shouldn't convert too soon. See Chapter 19 on handling IRAs and Roths after a death.) Other special benefits may also be available when the spouse is named as the sole beneficiary for a Roth or IRA account.

Surviving spouses who convert an inherited Roth account to their own aren't required to take distributions during their lifetimes.

QTIP Trusts

Most states have a Uniform Principal and Income Act defining how much of a distribution received by a trust is principal and how much is income. Qualified Terminable Interest (QTIP) trusts are designed to qualify for the federal estate tax marital deduction. The trust income is required to be distributed to the surviving spouse each year. If the retirement account provides information about the internal income of the fund to the trustee, the trustee must determine whether the internal income should be distributable as such. In other words, the amount to distribute for the plan may be the greater of the required minimum distribution or the income of the account. Amounts of income determined by activity of the account can be distributed as income to the beneficiary.[18]

According to the IRS, both the retirement plan benefit and the trust must meet the marital deduction requirements.[19] According to Revenue Ruling 2000-2 (modified and superseded by Revenue Ruling 2006-26), the governing instrument requirements are satisfied for a retirement benefit payable to a marital trust if (1) the marital trust contains the required language, giving the spouse the right to all the trust's and the plan's income annually and (2) the retirement plan document doesn't have any provisions that would prevent the trustee of the QTIP trust from complying with the trust's provisions for the plan.

QTIP trusts generally an ideal beneficiary for a retirement plan. It may be better to develop an alternative approach. The retirement account benefits are distributed over the single life expectancy of the oldest trust beneficiary, usually the surviving spouse. As a result, there is substantially less deferral than would be available if the spouse was the

---

[18] California Probate Code Section 16361, generally effective January 1, 2010

[19] Revenue Rulings 2006-26, 2006-22, and 2000-2

outright sole beneficiary of the account and rolled over the benefits to her own account. There may be other factors that would lead to deciding to designate a QTIP trust as a beneficiary. Consult with your legal counsel about this.

Note that no spousal rollover is allowed when the IRA is owned by a QTIP trust because the account isn't owned by the surviving spouse.

Named beneficiaries

If the participant/owner dies before the required beginning date (for regular IRAs, April 1 of the year following the year the participant reached age 70 ½; for Roth IRAs there is no required beginning date) and the beneficiary for the account isn't an individual, the account could be required to be distributed in five years. If the beneficiary for the account is an individual (other than a surviving spouse) or a qualifying trust, the account is distributed based the beneficiary's single actuarial life. (See Chapter 19 on handling an IRA or Roth account after a death.) If the surviving spouse is the sole beneficiary, the spouse can make a rollover to his or her own account, making the spouse the owner going forward.

If the family wants to extend the distribution period for the account, individual beneficiaries should generally be named for IRA and Roth accounts.

A trust can be a qualified beneficiary, entitled to the single actuarial life, if all of the beneficiaries can be determined on the date of death and all of the beneficiaries are individuals. The applicable distribution period is determined based on the life expectancy of the oldest trust beneficiary for the year after the death of the participant.

As explained in the chapter on handling IRAs and Roths after a death, required minimum distributions for an account with multiple beneficiaries generally are computed based on the age of the oldest beneficiary, but if the shares of the individual beneficiaries can be segregated into separate accounts by September 30 of the year following the death of the participant, the required minimum distribution can be separately computed for each inherited IRA based on the age of the beneficiary for each share.

If one of multiple beneficiaries for an account is not an individual, such as a charity, that share will have to be paid off by September 30 of the year after death or the account will have to be distributed within five years after death in the "death before required beginning date" scenario.

If the participant dies on or after the required beginning date, the minimum required distribution for non-individual beneficiaries is the remaining (single life table) actuarial life of the participant. This is usually better than the five-year distribution requirement that applies when the participant dies before the required beginning date, but a better result would usually apply with a named individual beneficiary.

The estate planning team should carefully review the beneficiary designations for each retirement account. In some cases, the participant should consider segregating shares before death to avoid an inadvertent result after death.

Conduit trusts, especially for minor beneficiaries

The family might want to preserve the maximum distribution period for an account, but not want to distribute the ownership of the account to a beneficiary immediately after the death of the participant. The participant could also want to control who will be the successor beneficiary for the account. An example is when the beneficiary for the account is a minor. A minor can't manage distributions received from an account and can't make decisions for distributions to be made from an account.

These objectives can be accomplished with a conduit trust.

A conduit trust is a trust that requires that all distributions received by the trust from the decedent's retirement account must be paid to only one beneficiary and for which the trustee has no power to accumulate plan distributions in the trust. When such a trust is the beneficiary of an IRA or Roth account, the Required Minimum Distribution Rules say that the beneficiary of the trust is considered to be the named beneficiary of the IRA or Roth account. Therefore, that person's age for the year following the death of the participant can be used to determine the applicable distribution period on the single life table. When the surviving spouse is the beneficiary of a conduit trust, the required minimum distribution can be recalculated each year based on the spouse's life expectancy, determined annually.

The remainder beneficiaries of the conduit trust are disregarded when computing required minimum distributions.

A conduit trust eliminates some of the difficulties of other trusts that can accumulate distributions, or that have multiple beneficiaries. For example, a charity can't be a remainder beneficiary for the account and still qualify for life expectancy distributions when the participant dies before the required beginning date unless the trust is a conduit trust. Also, if death occurs on or after that required beginning date, the deceased IRA owner's remaining life expectancy must be used for required minimum distributions, regardless of who the trust's beneficiaries are.

In the case of a minor or an incompetent beneficiary, the payment of the passed through distributions from the IRA or Roth account can be made to the legal guardian of the minor or disabled beneficiary. The IRS has privately ruled that distributions for a beneficiary may be paid to a special needs trust.

The payment of trust administration expenses using retirement account funds doesn't disqualify the trust as a conduit trust.[20]

Grantor trusts

Certain trusts known as grantor trusts are disregarded for income tax purposes under the Internal Revenue Code. The trust creator or beneficiary is treated for all income tax purposes as if that person was the owner of the trust's assets. Such a trust can qualify as a beneficiary for single life expectancy distributions. A qualified attorney can design such a trust.

Charitable beneficiaries

If the family has charitable inclinations and sufficient non-retirement assets to provide for the successors of the participant, charities are great candidates to be named beneficiaries. The charitable gift is deductible for estate tax purposes. The benefits paid to the charity escape income tax. A winning combination.

---

[20] Letter Rulings 200432027, 200432029

Just be sure to have the share of the charity in a retirement account either paid off or segregated from the shares of any individual beneficiaries before September 30 of the taxable year after the year the participant died.

A charitable beneficiary for which there is some ongoing flexibility for choosing the ultimate charity to receive the benefit is a donor advised fund. Persons you name can direct which charities will receive gifts from the donor advised fund. See your estate planning attorney for details.

Warning: Doing this through a trust is very hazardous, but possible.

Charitable remainder trust

The benefits of a retirement account can be made payable to a charitable remainder trust (CRT). At the death of the participant, the IRA can be paid all at once to the CRT, eliminating the need for required minimum distributions. The annuity or unitrust payments can be paid to a special needs trust for a disabled beneficiary.[21] (The principal ultimately goes to a charity.)

A charitable remainder trust might be the answer to any possible law change mandating distributions of inherited retirement accounts within five years after the death of the participant for all beneficiaries except surviving spouses and disabled minors. (This change was recently proposed but didn't pass, and doesn't appear to be imminent under the Trump Administration.)

Prepare the family, executor and trustee

The time frames for taking action for the retirement accounts after the death of the participant are short. There can be long-term consequences for any missteps. The estate planning team should brief the family, executor and trustees well in advance so they know what to do to assure the objectives of the family are accomplished.

---

[21] Revenue Ruling 2002-20

The best planning is done when the IRA or Roth owner is still living. After death, the estate plan should be timely implemented.

19
Handling an IRA or Roth account after a death

The detailed rules for handling an IRA or Roth account after a death are complex and beyond the scope of this book. Seek advice from a legal or tax professional who knows the rules. A more detailed helpful reference is *Inheriting An IRA*, by Michael J. Jones, CPA.

The time frame for many of the actions that are necessary can be very short, especially for a family that is grieving and may not be giving prompt attention to financial matters. The plan administrators aren't proactive in getting the accounts settled and the executor and trustee usually don't have authority to administer retirement accounts.

Here are some tips for handling retirement accounts after a death.

(The required beginning date is the date the plan participant must start taking distributions – usually April 1 of the year following the year the participant reaches age 70 ½ for accounts other than Roth IRA accounts. Roth IRA accounts don't have a required beginning date.)

1. Remember that the required minimum distribution for the year of death must be distributed to a beneficiary by December 31 of the year of death. (Avoid a 50% penalty for failing the make the distribution.)

   If a spousal rollover is made before making the required minimum distribution, there could be two penalties: one for failing to make a required minimum distribution, a second for making an excess contribution to the account of the surviving spouse!

2. In most cases, the IRA is distributable to a named beneficiary, not as directed in a will or trust. If there is no named beneficiary, see the plan documents or IRA adoption agreement.

3. Watch spousal rollovers or converting accounts to the surviving spouse's name. If the surviving spouse is under age 59 ½, death benefits can be made from a survivor "inherited" account, but not from an account in the surviving spouse's name.[22] A surviving spouse who is the sole beneficiary of a deceased spouse's account can convert it to his or her own name any time later.

4. An inherited 401(k) can be converted to a Roth by direct transfer after death. An inherited IRA can't be converted to a Roth. (Crazy!)[23]

5. If a QTIP election is made for a trust for the benefit of the surviving spouse which is named as the beneficiary of a retirement account, the election must be made for both the retirement account and the marital trust.[24] Both the retirement plan benefit and the trust must meet the marital deduction requirements, so the spouse must have the right to all the trust's and the plan's income annually. Minimum required distributions of a QTIP trust are paid based on the single life expectancy of the oldest beneficiary, usually the surviving spouse. If the QTIP trust qualifies as a conduit trust, the required minimum distribution should be computed based on the life expectancy of the surviving spouse, with annual recalculation. QTIP trusts must annually distribute the greater of the minimum required distribution for an IRA or the internal income of the IRA.

6. Remember beneficiaries are required to take required minimum distributions from Roth accounts. Since a non-beneficiary decedent was not required to take distributions, this is an easy item to miss.[25]

---

[22] Internal Revenue Code Section 72(t)(2)(A)(ii)

[23] Treasury Regulations Section 1.408-A-10, A-7, Notice 2009-75. Internal Revenue Code Section 408(d)(3)(C)

[24] Revenue Rulings 2006-26 and 2000-2

[25] Internal Revenue Code Section 408A(c)(5), Treasury Regulations Section 1.408A-6, A-14(b)

7. Special rules apply when a trust is a beneficiary of a retirement account and the participant died before his or her required beginning date. The account might be distributable within 5 years after death unless the beneficiaries' lives are ascertainable and other requirements are met.[26] It may be that adjustments need to be made, including making disclaimers or dividing accounts to separate beneficiaries, within 9 months after death. The deadline to have the accounts segregated and designated beneficiaries identified is September 30 of the year after the participant's death. The deadline for providing trust documentation for post-death distributions to the plan administrator is October 31 of the year after the participant's death.[27]

8. If the participant died before his or her required beginning date and there was no designated beneficiary for the account (including having the estate as the beneficiary), the account must be distributed by December 31 of the year that contains the fifth anniversary of the participant's date of death. Under the five-year distribution rule, annual distributions aren't required.[28]

   Note that, since there is no required beginning date for a Roth IRA, the five-year rule will always apply if there is no designated beneficiary for a Roth IRA.[29] If there is a designated beneficiary for a Roth IRA, minimum required distributions apply to the designated beneficiary, based on his or her life expectancy.[30]

9. Except for the surviving spouse, benefits are generally distributable over the actuarial single life of the named beneficiary or the oldest beneficiary of a trust from IRS tables the year after death, without recalculation (even after the death

---

[26] Treasury Regulations Section 1.401(a)(9)-3, A-2 & A-4
[27] Treasury Regulations Section 1.401(a)(9)-4
[28] Internal Revenue Code Section 401(a)(9)(B)(ii), Treasury Regulations Sections 1.401(a)(9)-3, A-2 and A-4
[29] Internal Revenue Code Section 408A(c)(5)
[30] Treasury Regulation Section 1.408A-6, A-14(b)

of the beneficiary).[31] If the account was in pay status (after the owner reached age 70 ½), the decedent's single life expectancy without recalculation can be used if it results in a longer distribution schedule.

Surviving spouse distributions for an inherited account are single life, with recalculation.[32] After a rollover or conversion to the surviving spouse's own account, distributions are required after the surviving spouse reaches age 70 ½, according to the usual rules. (Double life expectancy.)[33]

The required beginning date for the surviving spouse for an inherited account is the year after the participant's death if the participant died on or after his or her required beginning date.[34] If the participant died before his or her required beginning date, the required commencement date for the surviving spouse as a sole beneficiary is the later of the year following the year in which the participant died or the year in which the participant would have reached age 70 ½.[35]

10. A distribution will have to be made to a successor beneficiary (with the exception of a surviving spouse sole beneficiary when the decedent died before his or her required beginning date) by December 31 of the year after death and annually thereafter.[36] There is a potential 50% penalty for failure to distribute.[37]

11. Nonspouse beneficiaries can't rollover inherited IRAs, Roths or retirement accounts to their own account, but can make a direct transfer to an "inherited" account, for which they are named as the beneficiary.[38]

---

[31] Treasury Regulation Section 1.401(a)(9)-5, A-5(c)(1)
[32] Treasury Regulation Section 1.408-8, A-5(a)
[33] Treasury Regulation Section 1.408-8, A-7
[34] Treasury Regulation Section 1.401(a)(9)-2, A-5
[35] Treasury Regulation Section 1.401(a)(9)-3, A-3(b)
[36] Treasury Regulation Section 1.401(a)(9)-3, A-3
[37] Internal Revenue Code Section 4974(a)
[38] Internal Revenue Code Sections 402(c)(9), 408(d)(3)(C), 402(c)(11)(A)

12. Under the California Probate Code, only 10% of retirement plan distributions are allocated to income.[39] This may result in part of the income being retained by the trust that is needed by the income beneficiaries and the income being taxed to the trust based on its compressed federal income rate schedule. (There can be family arguments about these payments.) This rule doesn't apply to QTIP trusts. (See the section on QTIP Trusts in the chapter on Estate Planning for IRAs and Roths.) Also, a lump sum payment under the "five year" distribution rule for beneficiaries that aren't individuals is 100% principal.

[39] California Probate Code Section 16361(c)

20
Divorce

Federal tax laws have been fashioned to enable divorcing spouses to separate their assets without incurring a tax liability.

Same sex married couples are now subject to the same rules as other married couples after the Supreme Court's rulings in *United States v. Windsor*[40] and *Obergefell v. Hodges.*[41]

Registered domestic partners don't currently qualify for this relief because their relationship isn't a marriage.

An error in handling a division of retirement accounts can be very costly. The tax may be accelerated and may apply to the participant spouse, not the recipient spouse. Penalties for early distributions can apply.

To avoid these consequences, the division should be handled by a skilled family law attorney, possibly together with a tax advisor who knows the rules in this area.

Qualified Plans

For qualified plan accounts, such as 401(k), profit sharing plans, and government and retirement plans of tax exempt entities, the account can be divided without tax or penalty using a Qualified Domestic Relations Order, or QDRO. The QDRO requirements are defined at Internal Revenue Code Sections 401(a)(13)(B) and 414(p).

A QDRO is a judgment, decree or order, including approval of a property settlement agreement made according to a state's domestic relations or community property law and relating to the provision of child support, alimony or marital property rights to a spouse, former spouse, child or other dependent of a plan participant, meeting certain form requirements. The QDRO must specify the number of payments or the period to which the order applies.

---

[40] *United States v. Windsor*, 2013-2 USTC ¶ 60,667, June 26, 2013

[41] *Obergefell v. Hodges*, 2015-1 USTC ¶ 50,357, June 26, 2015

The IRS has provided sample language for a QDRO in Notice 97-11.

The QDRO is the documentation needed by the plan administrator to effect the division of the account.

Once the account is divided, the account received by the divorcing spouse is owned by him or her, and benefits can be based on his or her life expectancy, but the distribution for some qualified retirement plans may be based on the life expectancy of the plan participant.

There is an exception from the penalty for distributions before age 59 ½ when a divorcing spouse receives benefits under a QDRO, so a divorcing spouse can receive penalty-free distributions before age 59 ½.[42]

The terms of the plan may restrict when benefits can begin to a divorcing spouse. However, an order will qualify even though it provides that payments to the alternate payee may begin on or after the date on which the participant attains the earliest retirement age under the plan, whether or not the participant actually retires on that date.

If in-service distributions are permitted to the plan participant, the former spouse can receive in-service distributions to the same extent as the plan participant.

Distributions to a former spouse under a QDRO are taxable to the former spouse. Distributions to another person, such as a child or dependent, are taxable to the plan participant.

IRAs and Roth IRAs

Although the QDRO rules don't apply to IRAs and Roth IRAs, the transfer of these accounts to a spouse or former spouse under a divorce or separation agreement is nontaxable.[43]

For tax years before 2019, the rules for divorce or separation agreements are similar to those that apply for the alimony/spousal support deduction.[44] Since the alimony/spousal support deduction was repealed

[42] Internal Revenue Code Section 72(t)(2)(C)
[43] Internal Revenue Code Section 408(d)(6)
[44] Internal Revenue Code Section 71(b)(2)

by the Tax Cuts and Jobs Act of 2017 (except under grandfathered agreements), Congress changed the reference for divorce and separation agreements to the subsection on divorce for the exclusion from sale of gain for a principal residence.[45]

The transferred account is considered to be the IRA or Roth IRA account of the transferee spouse, so the rules for required distributions for them will be the same as for their other accounts.

Unlike qualified retirement plans, there is no exception to the penalty for distributions before reaching age 59 ½ for an IRA received by a spouse or former spouse under a divorce or separation agreement. The transferee spouse may qualify to take penalty-free distributions under an alternative exception, such as a series of substantially equal periodic payments.[46]

---

[45] Internal Revenue Code Section 121(d)(3)(C)(i)

[46] Internal Revenue Code Section 72(t)(2)(A)(iv)

21
Additional references

IRS forms and instructions (available at www.irs.gov)
Form 990-T – Exempt Organization Business Income Tax Return

Form 990-W – Estimated Tax on Unrelated Business Taxable Income for Tax-Exempt Organizations

Form 5305-A-SEP – Salary Reduction and Other Elective Simplified Employee Pension – Individual Retirement Accounts Contribution Agreement

Form 5305-SEP – Simplified Employee Pension – Individual Retirement Accounts Contribution Agreement

Form 5329 – Additional taxes on Qualified Plans (including IRAs) and Other Tax-Favored Accounts

Form 5330 – Return of Excise Taxes Relating to Employee Benefit Plans (excise tax on prohibited transactions)

Form 5500 Instructions (form may only be efiled) – Annual Return/Report of Employee Benefit Plan

Form 5500EZ – Annual Return of One Person (Owners and their Spouses) Retirement Plan

Form 5500SF Instructions (form may only be efiled) – Short Form Annual Return/Report of Small Employee Benefit Plan

Form 8606 – Nondeductible IRAs

Form 8880 – Credit for Qualified Retirement Savings Contributions

IRS Publications
Publication 560 – Retirement Plans For Small Businesses (SEP, SIMPLE and Qualified Plans)

Publication 575 – Pension and Annuity Income

Publication 590-A – Contributions to Individual Retirement Arrangements (IRAs)

Publication 590-B – Distributions from Individual Retirement Arrangements (IRAs)

Publication 598 – Tax On Unrelated Business Income of Exempt Organizations

Publication 4333 – SEP Retirement Plans For Small Businesses

Publication 4334 – SIMPLE IRA Plans for Small Businesses

Publication 4587 – Payroll Deduction IRAs For Small Businesses

Publication 4703 – Retirement Savings Contributions Credit

<u>Books</u>

The 2018 Pension Answer Book by Stephen J. Krass, Esq., Wolters Kluwer Law & Business

Life and Death Planning for Retirement Benefits, 7th Edition by Natalie Choate, Ataxplan Publications

2018 U.S. Master Pension Guide, by Barbara S. O'Dell, J.D. et. al., Wolters Kluwer Law & Business

Inheriting an IRA, by Michael J. Jones, Paddleboard Press

<u>Television interviews about IRAs, Roth IRAs and retirement accounts</u>

You can find FREE video interviews that have been posted on YouTube on a host of financial topics at www.financialinsiderweekly.com.

Interviews especially related to IRAs, Roth IRAs and retirement accounts include:

Bill Neville of Entrust Administration – “Investing in real estate using your IRA or Roth account”, and “Making alternative investments besides real estate using your IRA or Roth account”

Lamarr Baxter of Entrust Administration – “Investing in real estate using your IRA or Roth account”, and “Making alternative investments besides real estate using your IRA or Roth account”

Tom Anderson, President of The Retirement Industry Trust Association and founder and former President of Pensco Trust – “Investing in real estate using your IRA or Roth account”, and “Making alternative investments besides real estate using your IRA or Roth account”

Michael Jones, CPA, Thompson Jones LLP – "Beneficiary designations for retirement accounts", “Community property issues for retirement accounts”, and “Handling retirement accounts after a death”

Jeffrey B. Hare, attorney – “Using a checkbook LLC to invest IRA and Roth funds”

Naomi Comfort, attorney, The Silicon Valley Elder Law Group, PC – “How to handle retirement accounts after a death”

Raymond Sheffield, attorney – “Estate planning for retirement accounts”, and “Handling retirement accounts after a death”

Phil Price, EA, The Price Company – “Qualified retirement plans for small businesses”

22
About the Authors

Michael C. Gray founded his CPA firm, Michael Gray, CPA on October 1, 1996 and sold the firm to Thi T. Nguyen, CPA effective January 1, 2018. He has continuously worked in public accounting since June 1974. Mike was a co-founder and partner in charge of tax services of Hubler, Gray and Associates from June 1986 through September 1996 and a tax manager at KMG Main Hurdman, subsequently acquired by KPMG Peat Marwick, from February 1978 to June 1986.

The areas of practice that Mike has focused on include tax planning for individuals, estate and trust planning and administration, tax planning for businesses, tax examinations, and tax procedure. He also assists other tax practitioners in dealing with complex tax issues.

Mike was also the host of a weekly television show, called *Financial Insider Weekly*. You can find back episodes at www.financialinsiderweekly.com.

Mike has given many presentations and written many articles on tax subjects, including for the California Society of CPAs, Silicon Valley Bar Association and Santa Clara County Bar Association.

Mike has been a CPA in California since March 1977. He received his BS in accounting and MBA at San Jose State University in June 1974 and June 1978, respectively. He is a past president of the Silicon Valley San Jose CPAs, past chairman of the tax committee for the Silicon Valley San Jose CPAs and past member of the state tax committee for the California CPAs. He is also a member of the Santa Clara County Estate Planning Council, and has been involved with the Executive Planning Committee of the Tax Section for the Santa Clara County Bar Association, and is a lay member of the Silicon Valley Bar Association.

Michael Gray and his daughter and webmaster, Dawn Siemer, maintain several websites, including www.taxtrimmers.com, www.profitadvisors.com, www.stockoptionadvisors.com, www.realestateinvestingtax.com, and www.financialinsiderweekly.com.

An article about the initial web site for Michael Gray, CPA appeared in the October 1997 *Journal of Accountancy*. KNTV News also featured a story on his web site in the Technology section of the Six O'Clock News, and he has been profiled in *The San Jose Mercury News.* Mike has been quoted in *The San Jose Mercury News*, *The San Francisco Chronicle*, *The Wall Street Journal*, and *The New York Times.*

He is the author of the *Real Estate Tax Handbook*, *Secrets of Tax Planning for Employee Stock Options*, *Employee Stock Options – Executive Tax Planning*, and co-author of *Employee Stock Options – A Strategic Planning Guide For The 21st Century Optionaire.*

Mike's personal interests include the study of martial arts. He received his black belt from West Coast Tae Kwon Do in May 1996. He has also studied American Kenpo and Aikido.

Mike appeared as a member of the cast of *South Pacific* with the West Valley Light Opera, which was performed during November and early December 1997. He received a director's award, called the Captain's Cape, as the outstanding chorus member. He also appeared in the West Valley Light Opera production of *Carousel* during October and November 1998 and was the voice of Florenz Ziegfeld in the West Valley Light Opera production of *Will Rogers Follies* during June and July 2000.

Currently, Mike and his wife Janet devote their Saturdays to caring for their grandsons, Kyan and Clive Baker, while the boys' parents, Holly and Dan Baker, work in the family restaurant, Marché Aux Fleurs, in Ross, California and some weekdays enjoying spending time with their granddaughters, Kara and Minerva.

Ms. Thi T. Nguyen, CPA is a principal with Koehler & Associates CPAs, Inc. in San Jose, where she is in charge of the tax practice. She joined Koehlder & Associates in 2010, after working with Michael Gray, CPA for 10 years. Thi received a masters in taxation degree from San Jose State University and also bachelor's degrees in accounting and management information systems.

Thi is married to Allen Le, who is also a CPA. They have a son, Lance, and live in San Jose. They enjoy spending quality time with family and friends, and travel frequently to Vietnam to visit their extended family. Thi's hobbies include travel, listening to music and watching romances and comedies. Her favorite television show is Friends.

Appendix A
Retirement Plan Calendar checklist for after a death

Remember to read the plan. Its provisions override the possibilities of the tax law. For example, some plans require lump sum distributions. Some plans specify the spouse as the "default" beneficiary when none is named while others may specify the estate.

By the end of the year of death

- If decedent-participant died after the required beginning date (April 1 of year after reaching age 70 1/2), required minimum distribution must have been made to the decedent or successor beneficiary(s) for the account.

- If the decedent was taking payments as a series of substantially equal periodic payments, required minimum distribution must have been made to the decedent or successor beneficiary for the account.

By nine months after death

- Qualified disclaimers must be done so that the status as of September 30 of the year following the year of death can be established.

- Planned status and details of accounts (balance, community v. separate property, qualifying for marital or charitable deduction) must be determined to make preliminary computation of estate tax to prepare estate tax returns or request for extension of time to file estate tax returns. Payment or application of extension of time for payment of estate tax is due.

- If multiple named beneficiaries (not of a trust) desire separate treatment, such as computing distributions based on their individual life expectancies, or some want to cash out but others don't, their shares should be segregated into separate accounts by this date.

By September 30 of the year following the year of death

- If the account is to be distributed over an extended period of time, the interests of any disqualifying beneficiaries, including charities, disqualifying trusts, or the decedent-participant's estate should be eliminated by distributing their interest or disclaimer.

- Designated beneficiary(s) for the account(s) must be established.

- Once designated beneficiaries are established, they should consider establishing successor beneficiaries in the event of their death, if the plan permits it.

- If the surviving spouse is to be established as the sole designated beneficiary, other beneficiaries should be eliminated by segregating accounts, disclaimer or distribution.

By October 31 of the year following the year of death

- Required trust information must be provided to the administrator of the plan or IRA.

By December 31 of the year following the year of death

- If distributions are to be made based on the life expectancy of the decedent-participant or designated beneficiary(s), the required minimum distribution must be paid. Does not apply if the spouse rolls over or converts the account to his or her own name by December 31 of the year following the year of death.
- For IRA accounts with multiple (qualifying) designated beneficiaries that have been established by September 30 of the year following the year of death, the accounts should be segregated in separate accounts for each beneficiary, permitting using the beneficiary's separate life expectancy instead of the life expectancy of the oldest beneficiary to compute required minimum distributions.

By December 31 of the calendar year including the fifth anniversary of the decedent's death.

- If decedent died before the required beginning date and the beneficiaries don't qualify to receive benefits based on life expectancy (charity, estate, non-qualifying trust) or the beneficiary(s) elect to not receive benefits based on life expectancy, entire account balance must be distributed by this date.

- Roth IRAs don't have a required beginning date, so the five-year rule will always apply to them if the beneficiaries don't qualify to receive benefits based on life expectancy.

By December 31 of the year before a sole beneficiary spouse reaches age 70 1/2

- If the spouse has been receiving distributions as death benefits from an account in the deceased participant's name, consider rolling over the account or converting it to the surviving spouse's name to qualify for an extended distribution period over the joint lifetime of the surviving spouse and another beneficiary.

By April 1 of the year following the year a sole beneficiary spouse reaches age 70 1/2

- If the spouse elected to convert the account or rolled it over to an account in his or her name, the required minimum distribution for the year the spouse reached age 70 1/2 must be made by this date. It may be two minimum distribution payments must be completed by the end of the year.

Appendix B
IRS Actuarial Tables for Distributions

SINGLE LIFE TABLE

Age	Life Expectancy	Age	Life Expectancy	Age	Life Expectancy	Age	Life Expectancy
0	82.4	29	54.3	58	27.0	87	6.7
1	81.6	30	53.3	59	26.1	88	6.3
2	80.6	31	52.4	60	25.2	89	5.9
3	79.7	32	51.4	61	24.4	90	5.5
4	78.7	33	50.4	62	23.5	91	5.2
5	77.7	34	49.4	63	22.7	92	4.9
6	76.7	35	48.5	64	21.8	93	4.6
7	75.8	36	47.5	65	21.0	94	4.3
8	74.8	37	46.5	66	20.2	95	4.1
9	73.8	38	45.6	67	19.4	96	3.8
10	72.8	39	44.6	68	18.6	97	3.6
11	71.8	40	43.6	69	17.8	98	3.4
12	70.8	41	42.7	70	17.0	99	3.1
13	69.9	42	41.7	71	16.3	100	2.9
14	68.9	43	40.7	72	15.5	101	2.7
15	67.9	44	39.8	73	14.8	102	2.5
16	66.9	45	38.8	74	14.1	103	2.3
17	66.0	46	37.9	75	13.4	104	2.1
18	65.0	47	37.0	76	12.7	105	1.9
19	64.0	48	36.0	77	12.1	106	1.7
20	63.0	49	35.1	78	11.4	107	1.5
21	62.1	50	34.2	79	10.8	108	1.4
22	61.1	51	33.3	80	10.2	109	1.2
23	60.1	52	32.3	81	9.7	110	1.1
24	59.1	53	31.4	82	9.1	111+	1.0
25	58.2	54	30.5	83	8.6		
26	57.2	55	29.6	84	8.1		
27	56.2	56	28.7	85	7.6		
28	55.3	57	27.9	86	7.1		

UNIFORM LIFETIME TABLE

Age of employee	Distribution period	Age of employee	Distribution period
70	27.4	92	10.2
71	26.5	93	9.6
72	25.6	94	9.1
73	24.7	95	8.6
74	23.8	96	8.1
75	22.9	97	7.6
76	22.0	98	7.1
77	21.2	99	6.7
78	20.3	100	6.3
79	19.5	101	5.9
80	18.7	102	5.5
81	17.9	103	5.2
82	17.1	104	4.9
83	16.3	105	4.5
84	15.5	106	4.2
85	14.8	107	3.9
86	14.1	108	3.7
87	13.4	109	3.4
88	12.7	110	3.1
89	12.0	111	2.9
90	11.4	112	2.6
91	10.8	113	2.4
92	10.2	114	2.1
93	9.6	115+	1.9

Joint and last survivor expectancy table when one spouse is more than 10 calendar years younger than the other

See Appendix C of Publication 590-B. You can get it at www.irs.gov. The table is too big to print here.

98619007R00057

Made in the USA
Columbia, SC
28 June 2018